IN PURSUIT OF GODLINESS

IN PURSUIT OF GODLINESS

35 YEARS WITHOUT SEX

AARON APPIAH-KUBI

XULON PRESS ELITE

Xulon Press
2301 Lucien Way #415
Maitland, FL 32751
407.339.4217
www.xulonpress.com

Printed in the United States of America.

ISBN-13: 978-1-6305-0511-0

DEDICATION

This book is dedicated to the Almighty God, and His power of predestination which brought me into union with my wife. The amazing work of His Spirit kept us pure and guided us sexually unscathed, through a sex crazy world, to an unbelievable destiny.

To Him be the Glory now and forever more.

AMEN!

Not to us, O Lord, not to us,
but to your name goes all the glory
for your unfailing love and faithfulness.
—Psalm 115:1 (NLT)

CONTENTS

ACKNOWLEDGMENT

I want to appreciate the Lord God Almighty, who wonderfully planned our lives in such a way that the differences in our cultural upbringing, our distant geographic locations, and the different academic systems we found ourselves in, could not prevent our destinies from merging into His will.

I owe my mother, Mrs. Agnes Appiah-Kubi, popularly called Auntie Aggie of blessed memory, a mountain of gratitude for the extreme discipline, training, exceptional leadership and responsibility, and the godly and moral atmosphere she established in the home during my formative years. Together they constitute a trove of wealth that enrich my life on a daily basis. May the God she diligently served keep her soul in perfect peace.

I am also heavily indebted to my dear wife Sylvia, whose resolve to please God by choosing a godly life, made the objective of this book possible. She chose to listen to the voice of God against worldly pleasures. By opting for humility instead of glamour and prestige, she allowed God's will to come true for us. Her life of godly dedication became the objective end of an equally godly life of mine thus bringing us the utmost life of joy in Christ. (Proverbs 10:28). Her input is also an invaluable contribution toward the authoring of this book. Her offer to provide the material input for the Part II portion of this book and to proof read certain portions is also worthy of mention. But for her constant encouragement and reminders, this book would still be a distant away from reality.

I will also like to acknowledge my children Agnes, John and Aaron Jr for their demeanor throughout the period this book was written. Elementary school children as they are, they still exhibited complete obedience and total discipline at home and in school that gave us the peace we needed to think, recollect, search and research on the project.

INTRODUCTION

In between the will of God and the will of man lies the great Sea of Tears and Uncertainty. Every believer at a point in time will arrive at this sea where the waves of uncertainty batters the walls of hope, and the tide of fear surges against the coast of endurance. The promises of God fade into the far distance and one's ability to tap into them becomes remote. When we find ourselves sandwiched between the Red Sea and the Egyptian forces of life, we mostly waver, panic, make hasty decisions and accept wrong choices. We take matters into our own hands and by the time God's providence shows up, we would already be neck deep in the wrong choice, hundreds of miles away from the right path and so many degrees away from the right and original target. Once a promising soul, then wanders in dejection and despondency.

Welcome to the world of relationship! This is the land where many young believers lose their sanity and sanctity of life. I watch with dreadful palpitations, young believers surrendering their golden virgin trophy in exchange for wooden baskets of promiscuity on the platform of fornication. How many friendships with the opposite sex have not ended in sexual impurity? How many courtships have not resulted in pre-marital sex, an abomination in the midst of the people of God? It is always a slippery slope for young believers who are bombarded on all sides with sexual innuendos in our so-called modern world and culture.

How can we avoid this pitfall at all? How do we navigate our way out of this predatory and pervasive atmosphere? Be sober, be vigilant; because your adversary the devil, as a roaring lion, walketh about, seeking whom he may devour (1 Peter 5:8). This scripture sums it all. Believers, before you enter into a relationship, you must first cultivate the habit of vigilance, sobriety, godliness, thirst for righteousness, steadfastness of faith and purity of heart. Resolve never to sacrifice these principles for anything. In this book, you will learn how my acquaintance with the then future wife of mine progressed into a healthy friendship, to a godly relationship and culminated in a blessed, happy marriage. God took us through this long path of acquaintance and friendship for a decade and still came out sexually unstained, a victory that gives God glory and peace and satisfaction to our souls.

"For the grace of God that bringeth salvation hath appeared to all men,

Teaching us that, denying ungodliness and worldly lusts, we should live soberly, righteously, and godly, in this present world; Looking for that blessed hope, and the glorious appearing of the great God and our Savior Jesus Christ; Who gave himself for us, that he might redeem us from all iniquity, and purify unto himself a peculiar people, zealous of good works" —Titus 2:11-13. (NLT)

Furthermore, I have narrated how I laid a strong foundation of godly principles for my life by relying on the word of God. You will understand how strict adherence to these principles moved God's hand in my favor. You will also learn how my emphatic efforts at sexual purity was rewarded with a partner who was equally sexually pure, beautiful, godly, peaceful, helpful, respectful and lovely. It is a blessing I have enjoyed to this day. Did it come on a silver platter? No! There was a lot of sacrifices. There were many times I got frustrated, disappointed, confused and clueless. Yet, I held on to God's principles no matter what happened. In the end, everything turned out rewarding. It is always difficult making a choice as to who we would marry. Numerous methods of courtship have not shielded us from pre-marital sex, failed or broken relationships. Efforts by psychologists have yielded no results. How do we know if someone is the right partner or not? How can we be sure God agrees with our choice? My wife was someone I had considered impossible to have any relationship with let alone marry. You will be amazed, just as I was, how she eventually turned out to be my possible wife. This book was written to encourage you to stay the godly course in your relationships to ensure victory for you as well and glory to the Almighty and unchanging God. As He was in the days of the Patriarchs, so is He today working in our lives. If the youth of today could eschew fornication and turn their lives entirely to God, we could soon see our troubled society turn around for the better. It is my prayer that you take inspiration from this book and resolve to honor and glorify God with your youth. (1Timothy 4:12).

STAY BLESSED

PART I

CHAPTER 1

A CHILD IS BORN

"I am as a wonder unto many; but thou art my strong refuge."
—Psalm 71:7 (KJV)

Tucked into the armpit of the African continent is a country called Ghana. In the food-growing area of a forest district in Ghana lies a town populated mostly by peasant farmers. Two major arteries cross each other in the middle of the town: one runs from north to south and the other from east to west; thus, dividing the town into somewhat disproportionate quadrants. The north-south artery is a major tarred highway that takes travelers all the way to the northernmost parts of the country and beyond, while the opposite direction leads to the southernmost parts, right down to the coast of the Atlantic Ocean through Ghana's other major cities. The east-west road was mainly a combination of graveled and dusty portions. It led to and from the hinterlands and the surrounding food and cash crop growing villages.

This intersection is the town of Akumadan, a major tomato-growing area in Ghana. In the town's northwest corner, very close to the east-west artery was a relatively large compound. On this compound was a huge cocoa depot with a built-in office on the left-hand side. Hidden behind but walled to this big structure was a five-bedroom house with basic amenities popularly known as the "Co-operative House". On all sides of the structure were verandas and gutters to take away the running water whenever it rained. The walled space between the living quarters and the depot created a very wide concrete courtyard with a side entrance. On the left-hand side of this entrance was a kitchen followed by a lavatory. Close to the opposite wall of the quadrangle, a circular portion of the yard was filled with black soil ostensibly used for the growing of plants. Inside the black soil grew an apple tree which had overgrown both the wall and the quarters but not the high-roofed depot. Behind the quarters were some plots of land overgrown with bush. To the left of the living quarters was another small plot on which grew a big, old mango tree, the branches of which had spread as far as the rooftop. Further to the left was an excuse of a road that exited from the east-west artery, passed beneath the mango tree and gently sloped down toward the town's only clinic. Compared to the town's other buildings which were mostly built with mud and wood, these structures were built with cement blocks and corrugated iron sheets. As such, this particular building complex stood out as a relatively luxurious structure, at least by the prevailing standards of this rural community.

Inside this building complex lived one of the few prominent couples in the town with their three biological children and, a host of other adopted and relative-born children. Mr. Kojo Appiah-Kubi was a purchasing clerk for the Co-operative Cocoa Society which was the source for the building's name. His wife, Agnes, affectionately called Auntie Aggie, was one of the most enterprising women in the district with multiple careers. Previously a teacher, she was mainly into baking and farming. She was the leader and chairperson of the town's Bakers' Society. She also engaged in other seasonal trades such as the sale of bulk firewood and oranges and the petty trading of cosmetics. In addition, she maintained a provisions kiosk by the edge of the east-west artery, about three hundred meters away from her home. There, she sold all kinds of basic and household items needed by the community. These included bottled carbonated drinks like Fanta and Coca-Cola. She also sold ice-cold Kenkey, a pulpy drink made from a local delicacy which was the fastest moving item in her kiosk where she also sold pain relief tablets, bandages, GV paint, gauze as First Aid items.

In the evening of March 17, 1971, Auntie Aggie went into labor. She was led to the only local clinic in Akumadan, about a quarter of a mile away from their building complex, which was manned only by a practicing midwife and a nurse assistant. That very evening, she gave birth to her fourth child, a baby boy, whose appearance spurred uneasiness brewed in uncertainty rather than the usual joy that normally accompanies a newborn. The baby was very dark in complexion and extremely hairy at birth. Every baby, no matter which part of the world, usually looks pinkish in complexion and rarely will one find body hair. Yet, this child was born charcoal black and hairy. The hair on his head was very thick and dark as if it had been dyed in the womb shortly before birth. His face was puffed up as if he just descended from a professional boxing ring after a tough match. His eyes were rather tiny with thick eyebrows and eyelashes. Wide, open nostrils greeted everyone who beheld him.

As if these characteristics were not strange enough, the baby never cried during or after delivery. Auntie Aggie's three earlier children, like all other babies, gave a loud cry as soon as they were delivered. In contrast, this one came out without any fanfare. He arrived quietly with arms folded at his bosom as if to say, "No handshakes." He hardly ever moved his body in the crib except for the occasional glances of his eyes. All these peculiarities made Auntie Aggie dread what she had brought forth. This child was me, who, by the grace of God authored this book. According to my mother, I just lay there unperturbed with occasional movement of my eyes and limbs as if

I had been to the world before. She entertained the fear that one of her ancestors had revisited her which made her all the more uneasy. Should she treat me like a baby or an adult? Was I going to stay or depart into the ancestral world under cover of death? Could I be some sort of a spirit trying to have a feel of the human condition in the guise of a baby? These were some of the puzzling questions she had to grapple with. "Sorry, Mum. . . didn't mean to give you tough time. I just wielded my mysteries in my hands." God had His own agenda for me.

My mother went on to have two more children after me. Still, none of my siblings showed a fraction of the strangeness I placarded at my birth. With non-conformity symbolized in my birth, I understood, even in my childhood, that it was me alone against the world. The uniqueness of my characteristics was not only external but inherent as well. For instance, I grew up to be extremely introverted. Even one person was too many for me to encounter. I liked tucking myself into corners and enclosures. Solitude was my best companion. I could stay in a room or at any place where anonymity is guaranteed for hours and days without complaining. Boredom? There was no such word in my dictionary and still, I cannot find it even at present.

Much later in life, I moved into the home of an elderly cousin of mine, Mr. Nsonyameye, popularly known as Azay who became a father to me. I will fully discuss how I met this man in chapter seven. I remember very well that for more than two months since I first arrived in his house, I did not even go as far as the gates of the house. The conditions were perfect for a typical introvert. The house was remote and away from the buzzing of the city. During the day, Azay and his wife would leave for work in the city center making the house even quieter for my liking. Since I could get basic supplies (food, water, etc.), I would mostly stay in the living room reading for most of the day. I sometimes interspersed my reading with a movie. I also kept myself busy dutifully cleaning stuff indoors. It was the perfect atmosphere for me.

CHAPTER 2

FORMATIVE YEARS

"The rod and reproof give wisdom: but a child left to himself brin-geth his mother to shame."
—Proverbs 29:15 (KJV)

Growing up for me was interesting but mainly challenging. I usually found myself to be a loner. While other siblings easily blended in, I had a hard time mixing it up. I was extremely shy and kept a distance from everybody especially strangers. Anytime we visited other family members, it was a problem for me because I dreaded talking to them. In all these particulars, God had His own plan for me. He gave me unique characteristics which were mostly inherent and resourceful. Putting me into the world through my parents, especially my mother, was an exceptional plan the Lord executed silently. By their hands I would grow and learn so many principles of life naturally and determinedly.

We lived with other adopted children and children of the family members of both parents. One thing was certain. We were all sub-jected to the same treatment and had the same responsibilities and privileges. With so many children in the house, it took special

5

acumen for Auntie Aggie to manage us. Our ages ranged from under two to teenage, which made our care even more challenging. For instance, by 1975, my mother had had her last born while her firstborn was over thirteen years old and there were other adopted children who were years older than her eldest child. In addition to the extreme age difference, there was a spectrum of other issues for our family to deal with as the children came from different backgrounds and families, but Auntie Aggie harmoniously blended us together in everything we did.

THE CO-OPERATIVE SCHOOL

Living with Auntie Aggie from childhood was both fun and menacing. Living under her tutelage was a complete academy of life. This experience could easily be compared with a military academy where discipline, respect for basic rules, and seniority were the keys to our survival. No wonder life at the Co-operative House was nicknamed the Co-operative School by those who were familiar with our home. Later, those of us who were able to live fully in my mother's form of nurturing proudly taunted ourselves as graduates of the co-operative school, where only few students completed their courses.

ADMINISTRATION

> *"Whoever spares the rod hates their children, but the one who loves their children is diligent to discipline them." (Proverbs 13:24. ESV)*

Discipline was my mother's major administrative tool in the home. If there was anybody who exploited the above wisdom to the maximum, it was my mother. Just the slightest infraction would see her disciplinary hand fall heavily on the culprit. This made her presence one of the most fearful moments in times of disobedience. Her administrative acumen was never in doubt. She had a way of spelling out clearly to every child the rules that guided the home. She also designated to every child what his or her domestic duties were and the quality of work she expected from each child. She assigned time to every duty so we all knew what our duties were in the morning, afternoon and evening. From bed, everybody set out to work without waiting for further instructions. She always insisted that each child did his or her chores completely by him or herself. Any attempt to delegate one's chores or seek help without her knowledge was interpreted as laziness which she detested greatly, and the culprit always regretted miserably. Most of the time, some strokes of the cane would be administered as preliminary punishment while extra duty was added to the culprit's daily chores for weeks to complete a single punishment. Laziness and disobedience were the offenses that attracted the severest punishment.

My mother scarcely used reminders. She always insisted that we listened to instructions once and for all and keep them in mind. Forgetfulness was no excuse for not doing one's work. Once you forget, be prepared for the consequence because she would take no excuses. Indeed, life in the house, especially in the morning, could be compared to a formal organizational setup. Everyone would be busy at his or her post while Auntie Aggie would only appear once for inspection. We had water fetchers, those who boiled water for our morning bath, those who ironed school uniforms, those who swept the yard, those who disposed of the rubbish, those who set and cleaned the dining table (mainly for our parents), and those who washed bowls and cooking utensils to mention but few examples.

The house was very busy and full of crisscrossing movements yet everyone knew exactly what his or her business was. Any discovery of shoddiness would mean the entire chore had to be done all over again. Living under such conditions was obviously no fun, hence there were many who could not make it through the

Co-operative School. In our adult years, just the mentioning of the Co-operative School is automatically conjoined with the phrase, "Where only few passed the test of life." This was because many children ran away before they fully matured due to the extreme discipline and daily domestic chores required in this home. They would normally be found back in their parent's home. Some of them were brought back by their parents to "repeat their classes" because the parents wanted them to learn discipline which they themselves did not get from their parents or lacked the courage to administer to their children. Others never returned. The orphans who had no home or parents to run to were indelibly stuck with us, the biological children. There were times I wished I had a mother other than Auntie Aggie, so that I could run to her and never show up.

> *"Correct thy son, and he shall give thee rest; yea, he shall give delight unto thy soul."* (Proverbs. 29:17 KJV)

Conversely, there was positive reinforcement for those who worked diligently. Graduates of the Co-Operative School would attest to the fact that such training has been a catalyst for their smooth sail through the rough sea of life. Auntie Aggie made sure that nothing was lacking so far as children were concerned. Food was one of the provisions in constant supply. Truly, she always made sure that food was abundant in the house, but access to it was conditioned upon one's successful completion of his or her chores for the period. This made us associate food with work. Before we thought about food, we would first check if our duties were completed. If not, one would be sent back. That was a sure bet. There was not a single day with her when food scraps did not go into the refuse bin.

Occasionally, when one exceeded her expectation, Auntie Aggie would ask the person to make a wish and made sure it came true for him or her. Personally, there were not many such occasions for me, but the few times that I exceeded her expectation, I asked for a toy armored vehicle. Sounds like a soldier? Predictably! Clothing was supplied intermittently, but new clothes and footwear for Christmas and the New Year were annual rituals. Apparently, Christmases were one of the memorable moments with her. After a year of hard work, she always rewarded us with sumptuous meals, cookies and sweets, other provisions or gifts. Normally, this continued until two weeks into the New Year. The Christmas week up to the two weeks inside the new year were like vacation for us. My mother would completely drop her Headmistress posture and relax with us. She would give us more time to play, and there would be no prep time as on school days. She would introduce more varieties of food in our menus and supply us with new plates and bowls to eat from. We loved it because that was the only time we were allowed to accept gifts. After the second week of each new year, everybody's face sunk because life would have returned to the usual "let's get back to work" mode. I remember her making the following remarks in the Twi language on one Boxing Day when she gave us a lot of meals to choose from: "*Mepɛ sɛ daakye menni hɔ a, na moakae me,*" meaning "I want you to remember me in the future when I will be no more." And how true!

CHAPTER 3

MAJOR RULES AND REGULATIONS IN THE CO-OPERATIVE SCHOOL

My son, give attention to my words; incline your ear to
my sayings.
—Proverbs 4:20 (NKJV)

Life at the Co-operative School, headed by Headmistress Auntie Aggie was guided by strictness, military discipline, and adherence to basic rules. "Red" areas of life were clearly marked out. I would like to enumerate the major rules that made life at the Co-operative House a challenging one:

1. Do not eat or buy food from outside.
2. Do not receive gifts of whatever form, especially from unknown sources
3. Stay clear of accidents and incident-prone areas
4. Exercise restraint when there is alarm.
5. Beware of friends, or at least be choosy.

6. Never say "I can't" until you have tried it.
7. Give absolute respect to your senior.
8. Listen while I talk. Don't talk back.
9. Never collaborate with wrongful acts.

I must, however, make it clear that these rules were not written on the wall or in any formal document for us to learn. As infants and children, my mother chose to employ very practical means to teach us these rules. As we went about our daily chores, as we listened to our Do's and Don'ts, as one was punished or watched other children undergoing punishment, and as she reacted to our follies, we internalized these rules as a matter of course. Probably, it is because of this that I am still able to vividly recollect, categorize and explain them distinctively. Her methods of impartation were practical and classic. Through my growing years her rules got etched on my mind and still look fresh. The following lines elaborate what the above rules entailed.

RULE #1
DO NOT EAT OR BUY FOOD FROM OUTSIDE

Food was constantly in abundance at home thus making it almost a taboo to feed oneself from the outside. This, she made sure, was always the case. There was not a single day that smoke did not emanate from her kitchen windows. She taught us how to cook. In fact, cooking for the family was the duty of one of us (especially the older ones) at any point in time. Her strategy was to rotate this task among the older children from time to time regardless of whether the person was a boy or a girl. In modern day business administration parlance, we would call it job rotation, which is a major management technique for succession planning.

Contrary to the prevailing culture which designated cooking as women's duty, it did not matter whether one was a boy or a girl;

the same standards were expected. If Abraham, her second born, is now an expert in soup preparation and baking, it was the result of such prudent methods adopted by our mother to train boys and girls alike in culinary methods. The slightest deviation from the required standards drew strong, elaborate and sometimes exaggerated criticism. For instance, a soup tasting a little less than expected (given the ingredients) drew criticism that befitted a criminal. Afterward, she would calm down, sit with the culprit and audit the cooking process. Then, she would diagnose and address the problem. We always complained among ourselves that she overreacted to our mistakes. However, from another perspective, one could understand her way of thinking. We were under training, a military training so to speak. Cooking for the entire family (which she delegated) was her utmost duty as the mother of the home. She, therefore, bore the ultimate responsibility for any substandard cooking because our father would also come home and eat the same meal.

Nonetheless, this always kept us on our toes. With such conscious efforts to provide food for the family morning, afternoon and evening, she aimed at making outside food less attractive to us. In short, we always went out with full stomachs and came home to an abundance of meals. But why would she make such strenuous efforts to prevent us from eating outside the home? She did not tell me personally but the reasons are not far-fetched. As children in our formative years, our allegiance to the home was vital if we were to grow to become responsible adults. It is from the home that we learned basic rules for future success. On a practical level, as children, we could easily be abducted, drugged, or even poisoned through food by a malicious person.

Moreover, through food, we could be easily lured or socially engineered into giving intelligence information to outsiders who may use it for the wrong reasons. Again, buying food from outside was the easy way out, a situation she detested and interpreted as laziness. In addition, it is more expensive eating from the outside than cooking for oneself as she always made us understand. Buying ingredients and cooking for oneself saves some money. It was, therefore, vital that these threats that could result from eating from outside were kept at minimum hence the prohibition from eating from outside sources.

RULE #2
DO NOT RECEIVE GIFTS OF WHATEVER FORM, ESPECIALLY FROM UNKNOWN SOURCES

Another "red" area of life that was clearly marked out for us was the warning above. The simple reason for this is found in Deuteronomy 16:19b, "neither take a gift: for a gift doth blind the eyes of the wise, and pervert the words of the righteous." (KJV). Gifts (typically in the form of bribes) are powerful tools of corruption especially when it is money. Consequently, we were also warned not to pick up items, including money, from the ground unless to give it to the owner or show it to an elderly person if the owner was unknown. This clause put us in an exceedingly difficult position. Sometimes you would see a fallen money or an item on the ground whose owner you never knew. If you picked it up, and Auntie Aggie got to know of it, you were finished. If you did not pick it up, the next person after you would, and you would have given the 'opportunity' away. As a result, we were sometimes caught staring at fallen items and engaged in a mental debate until we finally gave up and walked on. After all, it was better to lose it to somebody else than to fall into the punitive hands of Auntie Aggie. Safety first!

RULE #3
STAY CLEAR OF ACCIDENTS AND INCIDENT-PRONE AREAS

The next caution of life, a domestic rule, was one that had external applications as well: *"Stay clear of accidents and incident-prone areas.*" By this rule, we were required, in part, to stay clear of broken glass, breakages, break downs, strange falls, destruction and construction sites among others. This was, however, a minor requirement of the rule. The main clause was to rush home whenever there was accident or we heard rumors of violent clashes in the town. Also, areas known to be hideouts for miscreants were to be avoided at all cost. This rule was one of those we greatly detested because it gagged our curiosity. It ran contrary to the behavior of the majority of the townsfolk. Whenever anything happened, everybody rushed to the accident spot to catch a glimpse but we were required to run away from the scene to our house.

I remember one of the many incidences that typified the application of this rule. In 1979 or thereabout, a Saurer flatbed trailer loaded with cartons of vegetable oil fell on its side at the latter end of the north-south highway that passes through the center of the town. Specifically, the accident happened in the valley of the Akumadan stream. Rumors of the accident quickly spread through the town. While the entire town, including our classmates, were rushing to the accident scene, we were frantically running in the opposite direction to the house from wherever we were. After a reasonable period of time, roll call would be taken at the Co-operative House and if one is unlucky enough to be absent, the full punishment concerning a breach of this law would be administered, regardless of how genuine one's reason might be. It was a "do-before-complain" affair. After making sure that all of the children were present, Auntie Aggie would then lock us in. Sometimes she stayed with us, other times she would leave to get more information about the incident if she believed it would affect our safety.

RULE #4
EXERCISE RESTRAINT WHEN THERE IS ALARM.

Closely related to the above rule was the one that required us not to rush whenever there was alarm, for most of the time we were kept indoors within the walled house. From time to time we heard bangs, unusual shouts, and strange noises from the outside. This rule, however, prevented us from moving out there to get close to the source of alarm. Anytime there was alarm from the outside, we rushed from our corridors and rooms to the open court of the house toward the main gate, but that was all we could do. At the court of the house, we would be looking into one another's face as if to ask, "Who goes out first?" From observation of how punishment under this rule was administered, one thing was clear. There was a clause which purported to claim that "copycats were not as guilty as pacesetters." That is, if one of us in such circumstances gathered the courage to open the gate and go outside, the rest of us were free to follow suit, because we would just be copying the leader. After the storm is settled, the one who first went out, thus setting the example for the rest to follow, would bear the whole brunt, carrying the sins of all the other children who went out after him or her. This punishment was so severe and multiplicative that no one was prepared to make such sacrifices.

In our static moments, Auntie Aggie would be very alert, watching out for the first person to go out in order to mark him or her down. She would give each of us individual looks and no one told anybody to return to his or her corridor, assignment, or room. Just a look was enough to communicate her command. Disappointingly, we would all return to our various domestic offices amidst glances and speculations as we grappled with what the incident could really be. Specifically, her eyes were one of her most effective tools of communication. In fact, she used her eyes more than any part of her body to communicate to us. For instance, if she looked at you once and turned away her face, it meant "be careful." If she looked at you intently and continuously, it meant "stop what you are doing or else . . ." If she looked at you from the top of your head to your feet, it meant "you are annoying" or "clear off." In such situations, one dared not stand where he or she was or continue what he or she was doing because the next step would certainly be disastrous. If she looked at you, gave a cynical smile, and shook her head in such a sequence, it meant "I forgive you because you don't know what you are doing but be warned." If she raised her eyebrows, it meant, "You are lying or I don't believe you"

RULE #5
BEWARE OF FRIENDS, OR AT LEAST BE CHOOSY

This was the next watchword that guided life at the Co-operative School. It seemed this was more of a convention than a rule. The punishment for violating such a convention was not clear cut. Usually, all the children were grouped according to age range, and each group ate together from one big bowl.

Nevertheless, if one brought a stranger to the house, my mother would separate the culprit's food from the rest of the children. She would then ask him or her to eat with his or her friend alone. Usually, the quantity of the food was such that it would not even be sufficient for one person yet the two of you would have to share it. Under such circumstances there was no room to act like Oliver Twist—ask for more—in spite of the abundance of food. Thus, whoever brought a stranger to the house went out with a half-full stomach. So, nobody really risked coming home with a stranger for the second time unless it was extremely important or inevitable.

This was something that I did not understand even in my thirtieth year. A few months before her death, I did raise this up. Auntie Aggie explained to me that picking people from the streets is not how we make friends. As children, we needed to get this right from the beginning. As she put it, "You don't come into my house with a person you just met, whose house you do not even know. I expect you to know the character of the person you are walking with. And if you will bring anybody home, know that the house is not yours, so I have to know it beforehand and prepare for the two of you." I followed up with another question. I asked her how she expected us to think so maturely when we were only children. She replied, "That's when and how you learn. If you cultivate a habit in your childhood, it would be very tough for you to unlearn after you have grown up with it. No one is ever too young to learn. On the other hand, you can't teach old dogs new tricks," she concluded.

It was not always that it had to do with food. Other times it had to do with household chores. One could realize, at times, that the tasks given to him or her to perform in the house were fit for two people when he or she brought a stranger home. However, he or she would be asked to do it alone thus giving him or her no time at all to play with the stranger friend. In fact, nobody got time to play unless at school where we had break time. In the house, there was little or no chance like that. Auntie Aggie always made sure we were occupied for a good reason except on weekends. For years, this had been her style. I quite remember she once came home to see us idle and playing a game of "draughts". We had finished our prescribed household chores for the period all right, but seeing us at play and not being productive is something she could not tolerate. So, she went straight into her room, took old newspapers, and began to tear them into small pieces. She then spread the paper shreds wide and across as she strolled through the backyard and came back into the main house, asking us to go and clean up the backyard. Even though we did not see her do it, we knew she had done that because we had just cleaned the place a few minutes before her arrival, knowing she would not allow us to play while there was work to do. Indeed, she was the first person who went to the backyard after we finished the initial cleaning, but nobody dared ask her any questions.

If bringing a friend to the house without prior notice to her was a problem, it was an even bigger problem when the friend turned out to be the opposite sex. One day, Emmanuel, her firstborn, being a high-school student, had a lady friend who visited. As soon as the girl entered, Auntie Aggie's eyes preyed on her son who was, as usual, undertaking his domestic chores in the evening. She brought a chair to sit close while the lady stood behind her son. With her fearful presence, Emmanuel could not even turn or lift his head let alone say "Hello" to the girl, as Auntie Aggie intently watched him. Worse, Auntie Aggie kept adding more chores as he neared completion of the previous one and the girl stood on her feet for several minutes unable to even chat with my eldest brother. None of us could chat with her either because you just didn't dare. The girl was confused but stood still. Then, brother Afful, one of the brilliant elderly children adopted by our parents, gathered the courage to go to the girl and softly begged her to leave or else her friend (my brother) may never finish his chores, let alone talk to her. Quietly, the girl left without being able to say a single word to my brother, her friend. It was quite humiliating, but that was Auntie Aggie for you. You either stuck to simple instructions or blamed yourself for the consequence. She did not give an inch.

Let me also add that any outing, such as seeing a friend, was strictly prohibited. I can easily recollect the few reasons for which one was allowed to go out—namely, school, church, errands, water fetching, and the farm. Any other outing, apart from these, needed her express permission, an exception of a sort she rarely granted. A single infraction and your guess is as good as mine. So, before we went to a formal boarding school, we were already familiar with boarding house conditions. No wonder staying at the boarding house brought no nostalgic feelings to me like my boarding house mates experienced. A few weeks into the boarding school curriculum, my friends would miss home and start talking nostalgically. For me, it was the normal thing, and I did not understand why they talked so fondly about home. I was having a break. My mother was stricter than both my headmaster and housemaster combined. Rules at my home were more rigid than those that existed in the boarding school. I always looked at my mates who complained with amazement. I never had any problem as every task or regulation seemed relaxed for me. I coped easily with every rule or challenge. I had no problems keeping within the boarding school rules. I never came home from the boarding school until vacation. My exeat card for more than five years of my high schooling still looked untouched by the time I completed. Once I arrived in the boarding school, the next time I would leave the gates would be vacation day. It was not until years later that I realized that the Co-operative School contributed greatly to my stability and success at high school.

RULE #6
NEVER SAY I CAN'T, UNTIL YOU HAVE TRIED IT

In this clause, we were supposed to try any challenge that was thrown at us not once or twice but several times before giving up. For instance, when one happens to be sent to a destination, there should not be any comment like "it is too far" before he or she set out. Obey the command first. When you come back, you are free to make whatever comment and complaint you have. Such comments would then be based on real experience, not on an estimate or guess work. In that case, one would not only be able to make the claim that it is far but will also be able to satisfactorily articulate the extent to which it is far. Any claim must have a credible backing or forget it. Auntie Aggie would not accept any claim based on assumptions. We were never to say "it can't be" until we had applied our wisdom and strength to the task before us. Any excuse for idleness was forever a non-starter before her. This, in a way, toughened us for future life that was obviously bigger than any of us. It generated a "can do" spirit in us and inculcated in us the habit of "never say die" which we would obviously need throughout our adulthood for the war of life. Those who did not take this rule seriously see themselves always boxed into a corner by life in our present age. They easily yield to an external locus of control.

RULE #7
GIVE ABSOLUTE RESPECT TO YOUR SENIOR

Respect for our seniors was perhaps one of the earliest concept every child at the Co-operative School was introduced to. Before one could walk, the family hierarchy was quite visible; accordingly, nobody told you where you belonged. Right from infancy one would know who was a senior and who had the right of way when there was a clash of interests. Auntie Aggie made sure that seniority was respected. Even if one is older than another by just one minute, it counted a lot in the Co-operative School. Any time items were being shared, older children took their turns first regardless of whether they were her own children, those of other relatives or adopted ones. Seniority by age came first. In a similar fashion, the older children were expected to take the lead in collective ventures such as fetching of water or going to the farm to harvest produce for our consumption. They were required to guide the younger ones to meet their scheduled targets anytime they saw them struggle with their tasks. Any time a younger one failed to perform his or her task satisfactorily, though he would be punished, the older one nearest to him or her who failed to guide the younger one was held jointly responsible. However, the latter's punishment was limited to a mere castigation in front of the entire household.

Nevertheless, the shame that came with such public rebuke was worthy of prevention.

The younger children by obligation, were expected to accord respect and obedience to the older ones. The major duties in the house were performed by the older children. They had the power to enlist the help of the younger ones in the course of performing such duties as long as the latter served as mere facilitators and not players. This type of help was mainly limited to errands and fetching of tools because no one could delegate his or her obligations. For instance, if one came to the house in a busy morning, he would find two or three little ones sitting in the center of the yard waiting for their names to be called. Their duty was to listen to whichever elder child called, go to him or her and provide the assistance the person needed, usually in the form of internal errand.

If any case of resistance came to my mother's attention, the younger one would be guilty by default. This sometimes gave the elderly children the opportunity to bully the younger. The latter could not complain unless it was so glaring that he or she was sure to win the case. Because of this rule, few reported cases came to her attention. If she had tolerated the multiple complaints of the numerous children under her care, she would hardly have had any time to concentrate on her daily engagements. Issues that won her attention were mostly cases in which the younger one was mistreated beyond a doubt and had a variety of witnesses. For instance, it was not enough to report that you were beaten by an older child. It wasn't enough either to have another child corroborate your story as a witness. For such cases to get her attention, one must also have physical marks or bruises that confirmed his or her story and that of the witness. If not, forget it. You will never win a case in Auntie Aggie's court of justice.

One of the far-reaching consequences of this rule especially on myself, is that it made some of us learn to live with our problems. We would hardly complain no matter how uncomfortable we were or where we found ourselves. It benefited us greatly when we started boarding school life. We were completely independent and sucked up all the mistreatment our seniors put us through. While other juniors were struggling and tearing up to cope with what seemed like a totally new and harsh environment, I took it easy and endured. The difficulties at the boarding house were nowhere near the disciplinarian environment we were living in with Auntie Aggie. Whatever we went through in the boarding schools was short-lived. When one is released, he is free for the rest of the period. At home, we woke up to discipline and went to bed with discipline. If things went awry, expect your sleep to be interrupted. That was a sure bet. Auntie Aggie would wake you up to complete an assignment that was 99.9 percent complete during the day but just did not have enough time or strength to complete the 0.001 percent. This did not happen in the boarding house. At least, there, we knew that when it is lights out, no one will disturb you.

Seniority was also greatly emphasized with respect to access to seats in the house. One particular caveat regarding seniority was that younger ones had to give up their seats to older ones whenever requested by the latter. If you were a younger child and you were asked by three older children to give up your seat, three times you would have to cede your seat without complaining. You would have no choice but to comply. This created a funny situation where some younger children never thought of chairs during gatherings or mealtime. We rather preferred to sit on the bare floor. Even so, the cynical older children would send the younger children to go and bring them chairs, knowing any resistance would be an offense before Auntie Aggie.

Another way in which seniority was expressed lay in the way we exercised choice in the house. Whenever anything was shared among us, the older children had the right to make their choice first, beginning from the oldest graduating downward to the youngest.

Unless an older child waived his or her right, no younger child could overtake him or her in the exercise of choice. No way.

RULE #8
LISTEN WHILE I TALK. DON'T TALK BACK.

This was the most implicit rule of all. If any new student arrived at the Co-operative School, it did not take more than a day for him or her to learn this rule. The way Auntie Aggie taught it was simple. Anytime she "had the floor" and you cut in, she would stop speaking immediately and give you an intense look. No one would need to tell you to stop right there. The feeling we had when learning this rule was like this: you would hear only your own voice when you ran your mouth. Once you realized you were the only one talking and every single eye was fixed on you, an eerie feeling would grip you, and your tongue would quickly stick to the roof of your mouth. You would feel there was something wrong unbeknownst to you. The other children would burst into sudden laughter. Then Auntie Aggie would motion them to stop. The place would be absolutely silent, and she would resume. As soon as you cut in again, she would stop. Once again, you would see that you were the only one talking and the same feeling would come over you. This kind of feeling was so ominous that by the second time, you would have figured out this rule already.

RULE #9
NEVER COLLABORATE WITH WRONGFUL ACTS.

By this rule we were prohibited from being accomplices in acts that Auntie Aggie considered wrong. Even if the person was one's biological sibling, we were obliged to give him or her up for punishment. Moreover, we were required to distance ourselves when the matter came up. If one tried to make statements in defense of the culprit or hide the facts to make the punishment lighter, he or she would receive double punishment as meted out to the culprit.

One incident which exemplified the application of this rule occurred on one holiday in the mid-morning. Around 7:00 A.M. that day, Auntie Aggie had returned from morning devotion at the Wesley Methodist Church. Being a holiday, she tasked us with extra household duties. We were charged to weed, sweep and clean the external compound around the house in addition to our daily household chores. After describing the scope and quality of work she expected from us, Auntie Aggie asked a couple of the older children to supervise the rest of us to do the work. My elder brother Emmanuel was one of them. The designated supervisors distributed the work among us, and we all went to work. Soon after, supervisor Emmanuel decided to take the opportunity, in our mother's absence, to make a quick dash to town. He just said he would be back soon and left. Unfortunately for him, Auntie Aggie spotted him in town from afar standing with a girl. She made a mental record of the girl and knew whose child she was. Then, Auntie Aggie quietly sneaked up on them from another direction. As soon as Emmanuel saw her, he took to his heels and left the girl behind. Auntie Aggie grabbed the girl and dragged her to her parent's home. As soon as the girl's parents saw the mood with which Auntie Aggie entered their house, coupled with the guilty look on their daughter's face, they immediately realized that, this firebrand, no-nonsense woman was up to no good. In order not to make matters worse, they gracefully received her, offered her a seat and water but she refused both. She went straight into action strictly warning the parents in a harsh tone not to allow their girl to play or flirt with her son. "The next time I see her with my son, I will whip her to death," she concluded and left.

Meanwhile, we were busily working on our tasks at home hoping to finish early so that we could enjoy the rest of the holiday. All of a sudden, we saw somebody sprinting like Carl Louis to the house. Guess who it was. If you said Emmanuel, you are right. It looked as if he had had a shot of adrenaline. He virtually collapsed to the ground upon reaching the left side of the house where we were working. He was completely out of breath and sweating. He had made the almost 450 meters in one quick sprint. The older children rushed to him and lifted him up to a sitting position amidst the chorus, "What's the matter? What's the matter with you?" Still panting for breath, Emmanuel could not speak. They gave him a sip of water and kept fanning him. They continued to ask him what the matter was. After about forty-five seconds, he managed to pull a short sentence through one of his exhalations. *"M'awu"* (I'd better be dead than alive), he said. Alarmed, the elderly children asked him why. Again, it took him some time to verbalize the word, 'Auntie!' As soon as the elderly children heard the word *Auntie*, they immediately left Emmanuel to his fate and returned to their tasks. This rule had kicked in. They did not want to have anything to do with him anymore. That was a typical rule #9 in practice.

Emmanuel still sat on the ground recovering while constantly looking at the direction of the approach to the house. Shortly afterward, Auntie Aggie emerged from the same direction and called Akos, one of the youngest children, to give account of what took place in her absence. This was her regular practice because my mother believed that babies do not lie, hence anytime something happened in her absence, she preferred to listen to the account of the younger ones first before the word of the older children. It was usually Akos, because she was the most talkative toddler among us. She would observe proceedings and begin to sing like a bird whenever my mother came in. After Akos gave her account, Auntie Aggie called Emmanuel into the room, and we heard the key click behind the door. It was locked. Seconds later, we heard the crack of a whip and Emmanuel's cry for mercy. When he said he was better dead than alive, he was spot on.

Auntie Aggie, my mother and headmistress of the Co-operative School in African Queen regalia. (1987)

CHAPTER 4

THE GREATEST LEGACY

"But Jesus said, "Let the little children come to Me, and do not forbid them; for of such is the kingdom of heaven."
—Matthew 19:14 (NKJV)

One of the greatest legacies and heritage my mother left us was a set of strong principles of life founded on godly fortitude. At the Co-operative House, church attendance on Sundays was compulsory for all. In addition, Children's Bible Class on Saturday was something no one could excuse him or herself from. Auntie Aggie would make sure everyone of us complied. Bible study and prayer was a daily routine for her. She also made sure this habit was inculcated in us, especially Bible reading and memory verses. Ability to memorize specific biblical quotations and recite certain portions of the Bible won her greatest admiration. For instance, at one time we could recite not less than twenty quotations from the Bible in the local language under the theme *"Nkwa Foforo Asempa"* (The Gospel of New Life). During vacation, every evening was for learning memory verses. Our elder brother, Abraham, was charged with this duty of teaching the younger ones as he was

29

given the outline for the learning of these biblical quotations. After each lesson was over, he would march us to our parents where we would recite our quotations]for them to assess the success of the lesson for the evening. Auntie Aggie would ask us questions to ascertain our level of understanding of those quotations. Sometimes our father would have it recorded as we recited and he would play it back to us. In a typical fashion, as young as five years old, Samuel, the last born, was able to recite over twenty verses consecutively from the Bible at one of the Akumadan Methodist Harvest occasions, quite to the astonishment of the congregation and all gathered.

Not only did Auntie Aggie enforce moral discipline among us, she also lived out a life of virtue that was so challenging that no one could ignore it. Courtesy was particularly important to her. She personally took interest in teaching it to us. She was a role model who inspired both confidence and envy in the local community: a hardworking mother who took interest in nurturing children the most appropriate way. She had a special ability in training children. This might have stemmed from her experience as a teacher. For instance, before ages six and eight, her two grandchildren, who were the last to live with her in later years, could tidy up the entire house and weed around it all by themselves. They could indeed carry out every household chore all by themselves even as incredibly young as they were. It was a matter of Auntie Aggie's training.

Schooling was as compulsory an element as church service in our days with my mother. Given her past experience, where she would have definitely gone academically higher if she had a helper, she was determined to push her children far higher above her level. There was not a single day she would not ready us all for school. Sometimes she would pay a surprise visit to the school to find out whether we were playing truant. I recollect there was a time in our school when my third-grade class had no teacher in particular. We constantly created inconveniences for other classes throughout the day. Other pupils also ventured into the bush and risked snake or scorpion bites. So, our head teacher gave our class an impromptu holiday and asked us to go home before the end of classes.

While all my friends were jubilant, I was melancholic. It was not because I did not like the idea; down within me I cherished it. My dilemma was what to tell Auntie Aggie when I went home. Since it was not a public holiday, there was no way I could convince her that we had been asked to go home early. Therefore, I hid myself in one of the stacks of cocoa bags in our father's cocoa depot. Unfortunately, one of the laborers saw me and reported it to my mother. She called out to me and I realized I had only two options: respond and face the consequences or pretend not to be there by keeping quiet and hiding in a more secure place. The latter was riskier, so I responded on the second call. I told her we had no teacher so our head teacher had dismissed the class.

True to my fears, she would not take my word for it. She asked me to wait for her while she went into her room and changed her clothes. She took my hands and literally dragged me to the school amidst threats that if I happened to be lying, I would face real music. We went straight to the head teacher's office where she inquired for herself. I was right after all. It was then that she accepted my story and we came back to the house. The arithmetic lessons she took me through and the exercises she gave me in the end made me wish our class had not been dismissed. My siblings came home from their morning school session to see me still working on assignments given by "teacher" Auntie Aggie. If I dreaded going home at the announcement of early dismissal, I had a case.

A typical school day looked like this: Wake up, brush one's teeth, do one's household chores, bathe, eat, dress and off to school. Auntie Aggie wouldn't give anybody money for anything. All logistics were provided so once your stomach was filled, you hit the road straight away. At that time, our schools were running morning and afternoon sessions where the morning session closed before midday. Since no one would have money or food on him or her at the close of the morning session, we would come home and refuel before going back for the afternoon session. After school, our homework was inspected, and Auntie Aggie made sure we did it. At times, she would personally teach us at home, in particular, arithmetic. A typical lesson, I quite remember, she taught me was the concept of the Least Common Multiple (LCM) and addition of fractions. It was a topic I found very difficult to understand in school. I came home one day, and she took me through it. She made it an easy job, and I finally got it once and for all.

Saturday mornings were also special days for us. She would wake us up at 6:00 A.M. in readiness for bible class at the Wesley Methodist Chapel. The Children's Bible Class was one of the ways that provided us with vital biblical knowledge, training and tools for godly life. My mother made sure we never missed such occasions. As early as 6:15 A.M. we would be on the way to the chapel. During lessons, tracts bearing the lessons for the day with colored pictures would be distributed to us. By 8 A.M. we would have returned to what was the most exciting about Saturday mornings—a children's radio program dubbed *"Mmofra Kyɛpɛn"* (Children's Portion). It was a children's radio program involving drama, songs and poem recitals in the local language. My father had a transistor radio (Akasanoma Brand) which he placed on the wall facing the court-yard. Adults and children alike would gather around it and listen actively to this very educative and entertaining program beamed by the Ghana Broadcasting Corporation. After that we would take breakfast. The older girls would do the laundry while the older boys would leave for the farm with the adults.

CHAPTER 5

MY ENCOUNTERS WITH THE HOLY SPIRIT

"And those he predestined, he also called; those he called, he also justified; those he justified, he also glorified." —Romans 8:30. (NIV)

As I have indicated earlier, I came to love God greatly. I got so excited at the miracles in the Bible that I personally wanted the God of the Bible to be my God. Reading His Word be it from the Bible, a tract, or other Christian literature was a delicacy to me.

As early as age nine, I encountered the Holy Spirit, but I did not know what had happened to me until four years later when I got the inkling. We were at a Sunday school class taught by one youth who also loved God very much. We called him Brother Obeng. He was teaching us the story of Daniel in the lions' den. He dramatized how Daniel would go up to pray in his window against the king's decree. Then he got reported and thrown into the lions' den. When he narrated to us the part of the scripture where Daniel had responded when the king called, and that God sent His angels to shut the mouths of the lions. the room suddenly became brighter. I felt a sensation I had never felt before under my skin. To date, I still do not have the words to describe exactly how I felt but the sensation was close to the following description: I felt like some warm water was being poured on my head and running over all my body and internal structures. I could feel all that underneath my skin. My heart became very light which in turn rendered me very joyous. When we closed from the Sunday school, I did not go into the main chapel building with my siblings and other children as usual. Neither did I wait for our parents to pick us up in their car after adult service. I went straight home and prayed in an open window exactly as Daniel did. I was happy to pray that way to the God of Daniel. My prayers had never been so passionate, meaningful, and enjoyable before. Everything I did that Sunday was excellent and enjoyable. I remember that I dry fried some peanuts and when my parents and the other children came to see it, they were full of admiration. It had fried perfectly and was very aromatic and attractive. Everybody yearned for a taste, and I was more than glad to offer them some. My joy on that day was beyond description.

My second encounter with the Spirit of God happened in high school. After my elementary and middle schools, I had completely imbibed the biblical way of life. I entered high school highly religious. I was tagged "The Boy with the Bible" because everywhere I went on the boarding school campus, I held a Bible my mother gave me in my hands. It was written in the local Twi language. I used to pray with the Psalms a lot. I joined the Scripture Union which was the only highly visible religious organization on campus. I was very punctual at their prayer and Bible study meetings. It was the only group that satisfied my religious cravings; they offered Bible Studies and discussions, prayer and fasting, biblical exhortations, biblical games, and Christian entertainment. Joining the Scripture Union also served as an insulation from the unfamiliar, somewhat bullying environment I had come into for my high school courses. I had traveled sixty miles (96 km) away from home.

One afternoon after lunch, I went to the classroom block with my best friend Francis. We chatted as we went along. While sitting in one of the classrooms talking about life at home and in school, one of the seniors who was years ahead of us, and who was the president of the campus Scripture Union entered. His last name was Akosa. As if he was sent by a divine source, he beckoned us to follow him. Like the fishermen and Jesus, we followed him without hesitation. He led us out of the main gate into a nearby elementary school block. We entered one of the classrooms, and he shut the door behind us. He then told us that we were going to pray for the baptism of the Holy Spirit and a spiritual gift, specifically the gift of speaking in tongues. He asked us to make a petition to God for it. I had heard many of the members of the Scripture Union speaking in strange languages whenever we met to pray, but I had no idea what that was. I felt more curious than confused. I had no doubt I was in the midst of people who professed the same faith as I had from home. Their belief and at least their professed moral standards were in harmony with my training and upbringing. They studied the same Bible as I had. I was at home with this group, but I was hearing people speak in unintelligible languages at our prayer meetings. This was totally strange to me. As an introvert, however, I kept my doubts to myself while trying to make meaning of what unfolded at our prayer meetings. It was therefore a welcome relief to me when this senior started explaining to us what the whole business of speaking in unintelligible languages I had been hearing was and how it came about. The second chapter of the Acts of the Apostles was our major resource.

After that we entered into a period of prayer. He asked us to be flexible and allow things to flow if we realized in the course of prayer that our language was changing or we felt like somebody was taking over our voice. The three of us began to pray together in expectancy. We prayed for what seemed like forty minutes. From time to time he interrupted and asked us how we were feeling. I would say nothing and Francis would respond similarly. Then, he would ask us if we desired the Holy Spirit. We would answer in the affirmative and he would ask us to go back into prayer.

The last time he stopped us he asked if we had anything to confess. I replied in the negative. Francis also responded in the same manner but was somewhat wobbly in his response. Akosa left me to pray while he attended to Francis individually. After a while, he announced that we had to get back to campus to prepare for supper. For that matter, we had to say our last prayer thanking God. I was puzzled because we had not achieved our objective so what were we thanking God for? Anyway, I was not going to argue with him, so I bowed down my head, a bit disappointed, and started thanking God for what Akosa had seen that I had not. Then the break came. Like my previous encounter, I felt some gentle energy in me. What was different, however, was that I prayed without my strength. My tongue rather moved faster than I would have it. I heard myself praying in a strange language. I did not understand it but in my heart I felt like I was uttering words of worship and gratitude to God. I was unwilling to stop praying even when Akosa beckoned us to. I kept rattling on as if I was being pushed from within. Gradually, I began to notice him as I slowed down. I did not like the idea of getting back to campus at all. At that time I felt like praying all the more. It felt like my lungs were filled with words of worship that needed to be breathed out.

We came back to campus but I was not yet done. I stood facing the school's outer wall and began making a clean breast of what filled my heart. I kept praying until supper time and still prayed in undertones. I knew the Spirit of God was at work. I felt particularly glad that in our next prayer meeting that evening, I would also be able to pray in tongues like some of the other students did. Surprisingly, by the time we gathered for the prayer meeting, I felt nothing like I had felt just a few hours before, when prayer had naturally flowed from my mouth. I expected the Holy Spirit to take over like He did then, but I was disappointed. I began to wonder what went wrong. However, from time to time I would go through that experience whether in our prayer meetings or in my Quiet Time but not always. Slowly I began to learn that we do not own the Spirit. He owns us; hence he rather instructs us not we Him. He decides to show Himself when He wills. We cannot invoke Him at our own will like the magicians and sorcerers do. He manifests Himself in His own timing not necessarily in accordance with our desires. It is our desires that must be tuned to Him and not the other way round. It was unfortunate that by the time I left campus, some members of the Scripture Union had not yet come to this realization. By expecting the Holy Spirit to always manifest Himself every time we wished, some members were led to speak in false tongues to their own deception. This is a hard truth but needs saying.

My next vivid encounter with the Spirit of God was four years later in the final year of my high school studies. We were getting ready to write the General Certificate of Examination, Ordinary Level (G. C. E. "O" Level) exam papers. For five years, I had been part of the Scripture Union on campus, worshiping God, studying and discussing His Word and praying. In my final year, I revved my prayer pattern up. I studied my books like my success depended entirely on me. When I got on my knees, I prayed like everything depended on God.

I had three like-minded friends who joined me for special prayers. After every supper, we would exit the campus gate and enter a nearby elementary school. Any classroom that was unlocked came in handy. When we could not get a classroom, we would walk into an unfinished estate house nearby. We would spend about an hour on our feet praying mainly for the impending examination. It was during one of those prayer sessions that I momentarily lost self-consciousness. Initially, I felt myself being filled by a vibrant but gentle energy. I started praying more loudly and powerfully. I was encouraged to urge my friends to pray with more zeal. After that meeting, I felt like the Lord had hearkened unto our prayer. We encouraged ourselves and went back to campus.

A couple of weeks later I took my first oral examination in French. I testify to the glory of God that I just mesmerized the examiner. I looked tiny, but my mouth was matured in the language. Throughout our interview, the examiner kept nodding his head. That was in the morning. In the afternoon, I was taking a nap on my bed in my cubicle. Suddenly, I overheard our student president relating to someone else how the examiner described my performance as excellent to the headmaster. He did not know the subject matter of his conversation was just a wall away from him. I lay quietly and eavesdropped with glee. That was how I got to know in advance that I would do well. I lay down quietly on my bunk bed concentrating on getting some rest before that evening's preparation for other exam papers. Half-way through the period, a voice kept urging me to get up and go downstairs. I got up and descended the stairs, turned toward my right-hand side and kept going.

I felt the power of prayer in my heart and started praying in a hushed voice as I went along. I was led by the Spirit into an uncompleted building. I entered one of the rooms, went straight into a corner and stood in prayer. Suddenly, I experienced the heaviest descent of the Spirit yet. I felt engulfed, overshadowed and completely overwhelmed by a powerful yet gentle presence who shared my functional faculties. I had no doubt the Spirit of God was at work in me. I remained prayerful after this encounter being thankful to God for visiting me. I went back to the dormitory humbled, sober, prayerful and reassured of God's presence. I began to feel that success in the exam was a forgone conclusion. God visited me at a time when I was praying for success in my exam. The timing was very significant because it was after my first paper. Knowing He was at hand to help encouraged me to face the rest of the papers with more confidence. What else can I think of other than complete success? It was timely and reassuring. To the glory of God, I testify that my results for this particular exam, were superb. I announce that with pride and gratitude.

My next encounter with the Holy Spirit was not personal as it happened to a classmate of mine. However, it revealed to me the personality and power of the Holy Spirit. This encounter was around the same time in my final year as we approached the exam period. The Scripture Union decided to hold an all-night session of Prayer, Bible Studies and Biblical exhortations. The aim was to solicit God's providence for the candidates even as the final exam approached. This was scheduled for one Friday evening in one of the classrooms. On the very day of the program, the leaders of the Scripture Union had gathered earlier at the venue to prepare the grounds in prayer. They engaged in serious and sweaty prayers. One could hear them from a distance.

During this period, a mate of mine, who loved to make fun of people by the name of Fokuo happened to pass by. He could see the prayer warriors through the opened louvers sweating in prayer. Realizing some were praying in tongues, he decided to go nearer and make a farce of them. He stood behind the louvers and started imitating the strange languages emanating from the inside when suddenly, he got "arrested" by the Holy Spirit. Like Saul when he saw the prophets in 1 Samuel 19:23, Fokuo became loud and unable to control his speech. He kept on "prophesying" until it seemed like he was being choked by his own words. He started panting for breath, unable to control himself. Someone saw his helpless state and went in to inform the prayer warriors about the situation. They fetched him and laid hands upon him in prayer for a period. When he finally regained composure, Fokuo was instantly a changed person. He became extremely calm, humble and respectful such that other students could not believe it. After this encounter, Fokuo developed the love for the Word of God and regularly attended Scripture Union meetings, and since then, he remained in the camp of the Scripture Union until we finished high school. I had experienced the power of the Holy Ghost before, but I had not seen Him so personified and powerful as this which deepened my reverence for God.

That was in 1989. The following year I gained admission into what used to be called the Sixth Form or the Advanced Level. Unlike the Ordinary Level which required five years of high school, the Sixth Form was a two-year program which required a decent pass in the G. C. E. Ordinary Level to be accepted into the program. It was a very intensive, elaborate, and advanced program of study leading to the award of the General Certificate of Examination, Advance Level. (G. C. E. "A" Level). A student with G. C. E "A" Level certificate needed two and a half to three years in the university to obtain a bachelor's degree. It was just a shade less than, if not equal to, an associate's degree.

CHAPTER 6

THE ACADEMIC WILDERNESS AND STAGNATION

"You let people ride over our heads; we went through fire and water, but you brought us to a place of abundance."
—Psalm 66:12 (NIV)

H aving passed the G. C. E. "O" Level with very flying colors, enrollment in the Sixth Form put me in a pole position for honors come the next two years. However, that was not to be. Instead my life entered a period of a gruesome trial of my faith, academic wilderness, a long bout of mental, physical and spiritual struggles, a sea of humiliation, a horizon of confusion, a swathe of despondency, an unending series of disappointments, failures and a long period of darkness.

I was shocked and perplexed at my first attempt of the G. C. E. "A" Level Examination. I expected a one-time pass, and a good one of course, like the "O" Level. However, all the papers I wrote barely passed. With a distinctive achievement in the "O" Level, my ego had shot to the clouds, expectations on the part of my parents, teachers and loved ones were beyond the stars. This had brought

41

enormous pressure on me, but I knew within myself that I was up to the challenge. I had virtually soaked myself in my books. I never went home at the mid-term breaks. During such periods, I took advantage of the quietness that prevailed on campus to rake in more knowledge in my subject areas and catch up on areas I had missed or failed to grasp well. I knew I was going to nail it but at the end of the day, it was a total disappointment. My expectation of ever making it to the university came crashing down. It took me several weeks to emerge from this hope-shattering experience.

I gathered myself to face the battle again, because I was convinced it was something that I should be able to overcome. In November through December of 1991, I retook the same exam. My results were still nothing to be proud of. Wait a minute! Was I missing something in terms of the syllabus or was somebody out there trying to sit on my happiness? There were questions I had no answers to and that exacerbated my confusion. I neither knew what other course books I needed nor how else I should study. I was overwhelmed by my inability to excel in the "A" Level examination. I drenched my pillows nightly and weathered my knees in prayer.

Despair set in the following year, 1992. The entire year passed without adding any academic laurels to my CV. However, I could not fathom going all the way through 1993 without a single academic achievement. I decided to do something to end the drought of academic success that was eroding my confidence. I gathered myself once again to confront what had then become my nemesis. In the middle of that year, I sat for the "A" Level examination again for the third time. What was previously unusual with me was gradually becoming the norm. It was another fiasco. I passed, but it was not enough to get me placement in the otherwise very highly competitive university admissions process. Looking at the prevailing competition, I did not even bother to put in an application. Slowly, I began to accept failure as part of my life. All this while I had seen these successive failures as temporary setbacks. This time it began to sink in fast. Since God would not listen to my supplications let alone reveal Himself to me as He previously had, I put the blame on myself. He was beyond doubt but what at all had I done to Him that He would not hearken to my tearful prayers and bring back the glory? It was a heart wrenching, spirit dampening, and clueless experience. Was He going to look on unconcerned while I dragged on in life with failure written on my face and shame hanging by my tail? Or, was He going to intervene at some point in time? I could not tell and I highly doubted God would ever spring back in my life. I searched and researched to see what could have been my sin in order to make amends to bring God back into my life. Hard as I searched, I could not find anything I had done in partic-ular that could have driven God away from me. That worsened my confusion.

Meanwhile, by the last quarter of 1994, my colleagues who made it the first time we attempted the "A" Level together, had entered their final year at the university for their bachelor's degree. They would be coming back to meet me still in the academic wil-derness in spite of the good start I had made. Some of these were friends I had personally helped in class. When they found certain topics difficult to understand, I personally taught them to grasp it. They passed, but I failed. They would come out to see this promising guy still unable to make it. How was I going to explain this to them? That thought alone was an excruciating part of the mental agony I was going through. Worse still, most of the tutors who taught me knew my academic ability hence they took it for granted that nothing was going to stop my march to academic par-adise. Therefore, anytime they happened to bump into me, their first question would be along the lines of "Which university are you attending?" or "What course are you pursuing at the univer-sity?" or "Which course did you major in?" or "Have you graduated yet?" That was a breaking point for me any time such an encounter happened. Any time I responded that I had not got enough passes in the "A" Level yet, the expression of shock in their faces tore my heart asunder. Their shock and disappointment symbolized the same loud scream of disappointment and bewilderment I heard silently within myself. I could virtually read the sentence, "You are a disappointment" in their faces. Whenever we parted, I would look back at them and admit to myself, "I let them down." That, to me was unbearable.

Such encounters and their subsequent feelings spurred me on for revenge. I began to see the "A" Level examination as my personal enemy. Conquering it, therefore, was no longer a choice but a duty. Academic disappointment was taking away my happiness and my courage. I gathered courage again in 1994 and tackled the "A" Level again one more time. Given my experiences over the years, I could not go in with high expectations, and true to that, another blow of worthless exam results hit me in the face. It had then become the pattern, so I was not worried as much as I was previously. I returned quietly home to the Azays. However, I began to speculate that maybe God wanted me to take another route in life, but which path I did not know. I was ready to attend the seminary to become a fully dedicated bachelor priest for His work. The critical question I asked myself was, "Was that really the way God wanted me to go?" I did not know for sure. God would not make it known to me either. It was spiritually torturous. I had bouts of sleepless nights.

In those days, I would get up deep in the night, walk out, and sit in Azay's car while brooding over my future and wondering which way to go. Azay once saw me in one of those agonizing moments and assured me of hope and brought me back in to sleep for the rest of the night. The following morning, he took me to a lecturer friend of his in one of the universities. He attempted to pull strings on my behalf. That too fell through when the lecturer failed to get back to us after he had promised to give us a feedback. I decided that life must go on no matter what. I had already taken a teaching appointment at a private elementary school the previous year, so I was thinking of making it a career and giving up any hope of academic pursuit. Although the ego in me kept fighting back, refusing to concede defeat to the "A" Level, I somehow concluded it was over for the interim. I needed a break. I switched my focus to researching other forms of pursuit.

That same year, my father brought me an application form for Teacher Training College where I could obtain a teacher's certificate. I abhorred the idea, so I turned down the application completely. I knew my "O" Level result was more than enough to get me into one of those colleges, but that path was not and had never been my ambition. If I wanted to follow that path, I should not have gone to the Sixth Form. I should have gone straight after the "O" Level Examination. Having gone through a higher curriculum in the "A" Level courses, the university was the original path cut for me then. Getting into one of those colleges seemed to be a bend backward. I quickly shrugged off the idea and resigned myself to fate.

One irony was that my academic brilliance had not eluded me. All other short courses I took, debates I engaged in, quizzes and essay contests I took part in, I either won or came out smashing. I just did not know what was wrong with me in terms of the "A" Level until 1999, eight years after my first attempt. It turned out to be a divine arrangement that was only meaningful in the future. God was purposely slowing me down for a peculiar reason—the best reason for my life as we would later see.

CHAPTER 7

A TIMELY REFUGE

"God is our refuge and strength, a very present help in trouble."
—Psalm 46:1 (KJV)

As I have previously indicated, I moved into the home of an older cousin of mine whose nickname was and still is Azay. It was not by accident that I ended up in his house. While I was wandering in the academic wilderness, I was also literally wandering in my physical life as well. From the Co-operative House, my father brought me to the city of Kumasi for my middle and high schools. My father could not afford to rent a hostel for me so I lived strictly in the more affordable boarding house. Therefore, lack of progress in academy somehow came to mean no clear-cut accommodation for me in the city. I did not as yet have a permanent footprint in Kumasi. Even though I had lived in this city for more than a decade, I resided in boarding houses. Now that I was out of school, my only means of stay was temporary accommodation. Many times, I was forced to go back to my parents in my hometown for lack of accommodation and food. My parents were still stuck with the larger family in my hometown. Until later years, when almost the entire family moved to Kumasi, whoever left Akumadan at that time was on his or her own.

Being largely independent even in early childhood, I kept trying to separate myself from the family in Akumadan and focus my life in Kumasi where I had been schooled for the larger portion of my life. Due to lack of means of self-support, however, I always had to return to my roots. The back-and-forth continued until I met Azay, who was then barely known to me. His name was quite familiar but I barely knew his person. I believe my encounter with him was a divine appointment as you will read later on. I was sure he knew me by virtue of my mother's popularity, and the fact that she was instrumental in getting his elder brother Yaw Opoku into the Ghanaian military. Azay was well established in Kumasi with various businesses. Dark, tall and short-haired, his name, Nsonyameye (meaning God will provide) had been completely overshadowed by the very popular nickname 'Azay.' What made this man so popular among the people whether at home in Kumasi, at work or in my hometown was his jovial nature.

To date, no one can converse with Azay for a single minute without bursting out loud in laughter. He has a thousand and one jokes in his head. He will easily find a joke and crack it before one finishes introducing him or herself. In spite of his wealth and popularity, he was and still is God-fearing, respectful, very humble and down to earth. Unlike many rich people who show off their wealth and money, Azay was very frugal and literally covered his wealth with jokes. He also dressed very modestly, mostly like an ordinary man in the street. He tactfully fronted his businesses with his younger brother known as Akwasi Baah. This made him very unsuspecting to many who had no knowledge of his wealth. Apart from the physical wealth, Azay was also endowed with a wealth of knowledge about life. He will joke with everybody but when he realizes one is serious about life or is in serious danger in life, he gets real. He will freely offer his advice to help a struggling individual, frequently fetching examples from the Bible and his own life experiences.

Azay was blessed with a lovely wife, Patience, affectionately called Sister Pat for her modest costumes. Short, thickly rounded and beautiful is the nutshell description I can give of her. Her protruding but beautiful eyes, graceful face, welcoming appearance and an everlasting smile will calm every storm in one's life. I first met them briefly in 1988 but I really got to know them in early 1993, in their rented apartment nearby. Even though Azay was very familiar with my mother, my uncle Brenya, and my brother Abraham, he was not very familiar with me. However, the excitement in his face during our encounter was reassuring. He urged me to visit him as frequently as I could. He also instructed Sister Pat to make provision for me during supper meals. Accordingly, every evening after they returned from work, I would leave for his abode and spend three to four hours with them. I would eat with Azay together from one bowl, read the newspapers he brought home, watch television and discuss current affairs with Azay.

For the first time, I had food security. Sometimes, when I got up, my only hope was supper and I would fast until Azay and his wife returned from work. Then, I would go to them and take supper and that would be my first and last meal of the day. One of my two major problems was gradually being solved. At least, supper was certain for every day leaving the temporary accommodation as my only major problem. Though our conversations were riddled with his jokes, I noticed that Azay was particularly interested in my academic knowledge and frequently asked my views and opinions about current affairs in our discussions. I have no doubt he caught glimpses of my academic brilliance in our discourse. He also saw this forum as the only way to get me to talk due to the extreme shyness I exhibited. This became the usual pattern as we got to know each other more and established a close bond. Realizing my need for a calm environment, he would urge me to occupy their apartment anytime they had to travel especially to our hometown for funerals.

By December 1993, the couple had completed their newly built house in another suburb, distant from the city hub. They would be moving in just before the Christmas of that year. I fell into a dilemma. Was I going to lose my daily supper, which was my only meal of the day so many times? Azay had become my only friend in the Ash-Town suburb where we lived, so how was I going to cope in his absence? Was I going to relapse into the back- and-forth life as I used to do when the going was tough? As usual, I would brood over such matters but would ultimately take it to God in prayer. I had not been to our hometown for a while since I became relatively stable in Kumasi after establishing a relationship with the Azays. I felt it was only a matter of time before I would be forced to return to my roots as the family prepared to leave for their new home.

I started preparing and psyching myself in order to wean myself from the Azays. Sometimes, I would not show up at all, and Azay would be worried. He would question me the next time I showed up, but I would give excuses. At last, D-day came and I was there when they packed their last belongings for their new home. My intention was to bid them farewell but Azay invited me to get on board to see their new home to make my subsequent visits easy. Sister Pat and their children had already been dropped in the new home earlier in the day. I hopped into Azay's white, big-wheeled, and highly suspended Suzuki Grand Vitara. We drove through the city center, the buildings eventually fading into a suburban environment. The area was a new development plot with sparsely located buildings, only a few of which were completed. There were undeveloped plots all around. The house was a five-bedroom terrazzo house with two baths. It had a very large living room, which had openings to the kitchen and the balcony in opposite directions. The balcony was also large. There was a high wall around the house with copious space between them. One could easily drive a ten-ton dump truck around the house within the walls. Even larger was the space in front of the house. From the balcony to the outer wall was a full plot designated for future development and it was all cemented.

After inspecting the house, I was full of praise for Azay and told him how I liked the house and the environment. It was very quiet, cool and had a serene atmosphere. Apart from the occasional singing of birds, the only noise in the area was one's own voice. We had a lot of discussion both on the house and on current affairs during meals. We continued until late in the night when I found one of the rooms and threw myself on the floor. I was gone in a moment into dreamland.

When I woke up the next morning, I spent much time indoors praying to God and considering the excellent environment of the abode. I loved the environment and intermittently fantasized about when I could have something of that sort. To me it was a perfect environment, one most suited for my introverted nature. I came out late as did Azay. By the time I ventured out of the room, Sister Pat was ready with breakfast. Shortly afterwards, Azay also emerged from his room onto the balcony, and I greeted him. We had breakfast and stayed until after lunch. I then indicated to Azay that I wanted to return well before nightfall, so I begged leave of him. He urged me to stay a little longer as he promised to drop me off. I did and he dropped me at my abode in the evening. Before he took off again, he strongly urged me to visit and spend the following weekend with him. I agreed and promised to be there the following Friday evening and would stay until Sunday. With that, we said our goodbyes as he drove off. I was very melancholic and wished the following weekend a speedy arrival. On the following Friday, I set out in the early evening for the much-awaited visit to the Azays. I spent the entire weekend with them. The meals, the chat, the music and the warmth from Sister Pat's reception were wonderful. Sadness began to creep in when it was time to leave. I walked up to Azay and begged leave of him. He asked me to wait while he grabbed his shirt. Together, we walked out of the gates as he saw me off. A few meters out from the main gate, he stopped and called my name. I responded thinking that it was the farthest place he could see me off to. I was ready to say goodbye when he told me, "I want you to come and stay with us." It was an absolute stunner. I could not believe my ears. I did not know what to say. I kept a stable demeanor though and gave a forceful smile. All I remember saying was the words, "thank you." He smiled back at me as we plodded on to the taxicab station.

That evening, I was full of gratitude to God for how His providence was booming in my life. For the first time within the academic wilderness, God was bouncing back actively into my life. I thought I was going to fall back into the old needy life with the departure of the Azays but God turned it into a full solution for my two major problems prevailing at that time: food security and permanent accommodation. I had never been so grateful to God. My night was full of dreams. Within three days, I had inserted myself squarely in Azay's home. Their commitment to me and my reciprocated loyalty soon earned me the first-born son status of the Azays in the eyes of our neighbors.

My presence in the home of the Azays marked a very conspicuous turning point in my life. I gained permanent residence in Kumasi, limited only by my ability to stay disciplined and obedient. The "Co-operative School" had made sure I had plenty of that. Perhaps Azay might have observed it in our interactions, hence that move. The Azays gave me complete freedom in their house. I could eat whatever I could lay my hands on, listen to whatever music I wanted and watch whatever movie I liked. Hitherto, these choices were quite remote and unaffordable to me. No area in the house was out of bounds to me, even their very bedroom. Later on, they put their vehicles at my disposal and responded to me with respect. They reposed an unquestionable trust in me such that Azay would periodically hand me huge sums of money in U.S. dollars and ask me to keep it. These were amounts I had never seen or handled before. He would not tell me when he would come for it but I made sure whatever sum it was, it remained intact until he demanded it, usually unexpectedly.

As a businessman, Azay traveled frequently. On each occasion, he would ask me what movies I liked. I would give him a list of seven and he would make sure he bought me four of them at least. I was very surprised at the kind of respect they gave me. Even though I was living under their roof, they gave me absolute privacy. I entered their room frequently but they hardly ever set foot in mine. For all the years I remained in their home, Sister Pat fed me daily and never raised a finger against me. Her husband never chastised me for any wrong I did. I tried to live as obediently as possible. However, if I did commit a blunder, he deemed it unintentional and that I was wise enough to realize my mistake. I never disappointed him or his wife in that respect. They demonstrated an exceptional patience and kindness toward me which gave me the needed space to develop my person and to learn a lot from them.

For instance, Sister Pat served her husband with godly humility and obedience. They demonstrated love and affection for each other in a way that made their marriage very desirable to me. They loved discipline and godliness and instilled these attributes in their children. A few months after I arrived in their home, Azay asked me not to hesitate to discipline his relatively little children in his absence if they misbehaved. Indeed, the atmosphere in the home agreed with my training and aligned perfectly with my way of life. I enjoyed every bit of the many years I spent with these God-given surrogates. I also responded by dutifully occupying myself with household chores. Teaching the children, cleaning the interior of the house, washing vehicles, watering grasses and trimming flowers, caring for pet dogs, running errands, and so on. We got on very well. It was quite a challenge, especially for the children and myself, when I had to leave their home to be joined with my wife. It really came to tears for Azay's daughters. That is how cordially I assimilated into that family and bonded with them to become one unique family.

In all these changes in my life, I saw the hand of God moving me along a divine timeline. My encounter with the Azays was not a random thing. Through them, God solved the most pressing needs of my young life. I picked a few ethical lessons from their friendliness and easygoing personality. I was quite the opposite. I gradually learned how to crack jokes. I also learned the value of patience from them. Perhaps that is why Azay chose to marry a woman called Patience. Azay was older, rich, and wealthy but when provoked, he would not react. It would take him days, sometimes weeks to respond to a single, repeated provocation. Quite often, he ignored them altogether. That was one fine virtue I picked from him. It enabled him to focus on his business objectives. No wonder he is still rich.

Another particular nugget from his wisdom that made a lasting impression on me came one day as we were chatting in his living room. I remarked that even though he was rich, his wealth does not speak as loudly as others I knew of, and that he needed to show off once in a while at least, to let people know that he is also somebody. He responded, "If you think you are rich, someone is richer than you. If you think you are wise, someone is wiser than you. If you think you are beautiful, someone is more beautiful than you. If you think you are clever, someone is cleverer than you. Whatever you think you are, someone is more than you. And even if you are the first today, someone will beat you tomorrow. What then can you really boast of or show off?" He concluded. I could not say anything anymore. He just drained every word out of me with that short speech. That day, I went to bed still pondering over his response. It took me weeks to digest such compact wisdom coming from him. By the time I understood it to the bottom, it had stuck to my mind forever. Moderation is still a high priority in my conduct everywhere I go.

My encounter with the Azays was not a random thing.

CHAPTER 8

LAYING THE FOUNDATION FOR MY VOW

"The Lord directs the steps of the godly. He delights in every detail of their lives."
—Psalms 37:23 (NLT)

Significantly, in January of the year 1995, the Ash-Town Baptist Church (ATBC) in the city of Kumasi, to which I belonged had an interim pastor. He was S.A.S. Boateng, a converted Muslim. He was a firebrand so far as the Christian life was concerned. He had previously been the Regional Youth Outreach Secretary for the Scripture Union in the Ashanti Region of Ghana for many years, so his face was familiar to me. He paid frequent visits to us in my school's branch of the Scripture Union. It was, therefore, no surprise to me when he focused extensively on the youth when he took over the reins of Ash-Town Baptist Church. His tenure of office was and is still significant to me because of the policies he pursued. He made the youth his major focus. He personally vetted our programs and took keen interest in their implementation. He introduced registers at Sunday School sessions where records of attendance were kept of each member to enable him track those who slacked. He would send the deacons in pursuit of such people. He would use every means possible to track and bring the truant fellow back.

One must have a very genuine reason for not showing up at Sunday School or else Pastor Boateng will severely chastise you. At first, I was not totally in agreement with this policy of his because I thought church service was voluntary as was Sunday School. In contrast, this pastor would rather have you attend the Sunday School at the expense of the sermon service. Later, I came to realize that I was wrong in my thinking. The blood of Christ was too precious to be let go to waste. The soul of each member was equally too precious to lose. Moreover, Sunday School was the only avenue for some members to have effective discussion of the Bible for an entire week. Therefore, missing Sunday School was a big deal for Pastor Boateng. Another thing I liked was his emphasis on the chastity of the youth in the church. He liked the theme the youth group in the church chose for that year, "Let No Man Despise Thy Youth" after 1Tim. 4:12. He was uncompromising on this theme, something that other youth members interpreted as harsh. Personally, however, I was all for it. It suited my lifestyle well and was my very goal for the future.

My goal was to please God with my youthfulness, whatever challenge it presented. I had long sought to prove wrong the widespread notion that abstaining from sex in one's sexually active age makes him or her retarded or antisocial in a way. This was a myth that was destroying the youth of my age. People used that excuse to willfully sin against God and their own bodies and still expected God to sign onto it. I was always angry at such obvious falsehood and deception. I could not see logically how not having sex could change one's biological synthesis to render him worse off. I thought rather that If I had all my juices and energy in me that should make me healthier and stronger than if I lose them. So, how could one become worse off? It did not make sense to me, and I wondered where that theory came from.

I got mad at the antisocial myth. It was a blatant lie that defied both logic and common sense. That made me even angrier and resolute in my desire to prove to members of society that such a notion was not only unfounded but sinful as well. I was determined to call the bluff of anyone purveying such a myth. A life of sexual purity must not result in a worse personal estate, and I was out to prove it with my own life. From the very foundations of my life, I had always distrusted society. I preferred being solitary to companionship. Therefore, if sexual abstinence could help me defy society, then I was all for it. I wondered why people talked of an anti-social nature in unfavorable terms. It was helpful to me and I enjoyed it. It insulated me from undue societal and peer influence, so what were they talking about? I never felt lonely in my solitude. I felt whole and completely satisfied with my life. I never felt like I needed somebody apart from Christ to make me whole. The Word of God was more than enough for me. I felt rather empty when I failed to study the Bible.

In Christ I found all I needed in life. Cultural and societal norms were very strong in my setting, but I observed one thing about societal norms—those who gathered courage to break them mostly did well. I did not like the idea of toeing a particular line in order to belong or to please somebody. I loved to be independent and enjoyed my solitude. This made me the more willing and resolute to stay chaste. I knew the Bible encouraged chastity and sexual purity; hence it would be rewarded by God. I liked it when it was challenging because it gave me a sense of accomplishment whenever I overcame temptation. It made me feel that I was overcoming for God. I held that view until I came to understand what the grace of God really meant. It was God overcoming through me; not I overcoming for Him. Though I have been rewarded by God in different ways, I am still looking forward to His biggest reward ever for my life. When you obey God, you should expect His blessings in multiple ways because His promises are numerous and secure.

Furthermore, pastor Boateng's chastity program was in line with my upbringing and orientation. Growing up, my mother used to distinctively separate us the boys from the girls in a way that was more respectable to the girls than the boys. When it came to girl issues, she was keener and leaned more toward them. In our teenage years, she discouraged us from developing friendships with members of the other sex let alone think of more intimate relationships. As an introvert, I took it in one hundred percent and somehow developed the notion that even talking with the opposite sex could lead to sin. This line of thinking fitted well into my introverted personality. Even approaching people was a problem to me so if I had a reason not to speak to people, I loved it. I only overcame this thinking in my early twenties when I challenged my mother on why she barely allowed friendships with the opposite sex. She did not disagree with my assessment but made a statement that still resounds with me. In her words, "Friendship with the opposite sex is usually blurred and seamlessly blends with relationships. And things happen very fast." I thought I understood it until many years later when I realized I did not grasp the last portion of her statement. I was listening to a television documentary in which a young woman narrated her ordeal in a rape incident. She used to go out with a young man who had so far proved to be harmless and caring. Their friendship had been incident free until one day when she paid him a visit. In her words, "A hug, a kiss and things happened very quickly." Immediately, my mother's statement flashed back, and I realized what she was referring to. I was so naive. For me, Pastor Boateng's chastity program was a smooth ride but for some it was a bumpy road.

Moreover, I had also observed with anger, repugnance, regret and disappointment, a pattern that went on in the lives of the adults in town, my family, all around and beyond. Fathers, uncles, elder brothers, and cousins, so-called men of God, government officials and more had all had children by women other than their wives. I did not like it because they all professed Christianity yet I could not see what was so Christian about such evidence of fornication and adultery. My spiritual life was gaining momentum. I burned with fierce anger as I searched through the Bible to find out any justification for such outrageous behavior. I concluded that it was a problem of society—lack of sobriety—hence they easily fell for sexual temptations. And they lacked self-control because they had not lived up to God's principles. What became of their Sunday worship and the big Bibles they paraded before men? For this reason, I picked a spiritual weapon from the Bible with which to strike at the devil on this subject: "Submit yourselves therefore to God. Resist the devil, and he will flee from you" (James 4:7 KJV). I vowed in my heart that if that trend was a train, it stops at my door. If it was a curse, the buck stops at my feet. No way! I strongly determined to prove to God that if He could not rely on any member of my community in the past, I will go to every length to save the situation. I prayed to Him to give me the grace to set the right example. I took personal responsibility to right the wrong. Fornication or pre-marital sex, therefore, became the most hated and repugnant subject to me. Staying chaste was everything to me if I would ever prove that point. I buried myself in the Bible, constantly prayed and fasted for spiritual strength to enable me reach this glorious goal. It would certainly be an incredible story to tell in the future when I shall have succeeded.

By the middle of 1995, Pastor Boateng's chastity agenda had gained full currency in the church. The deacons as well as other groups were on board. Members who could not cope fell out. A week-long program was drafted for the youth to commemorate a "Youth Week" in the church. During the program, the youth were educated on the reasons, benefits, and requirements of chastity in accordance with the theme. Sexual immorality and its implications were also discussed.

On the day before the end of the program, it was announced that we would be making a covenant with God. We would make a promise to abstain from sexual immorality until we married. It would be marked by a very small laminated paper with the abstinence promise on it. We would keep it as a reminder until we entered into the blessings of marriage. For me it was spot on, but the facial expressions of some members told a long story. I wondered what they thought we were going through all those lessons on abstinence for. The pastor, however, added that it was not going to be an obligatory exercise. With our heads bowed in prayer, the pastor announced that those who wanted to opt out could quietly file out to meet him outside. I was among those who filed out and I am sure the pastor was surprised as you are now, to see me among the few. Many knew I was morally unquestionable so what made me opt out was a mystery. Was I hiding something all this while? I am sure that was the question in the pastor's mind. In reality, I was not opting out. I had a higher objective than the current proposed covenant. What we were about to do was not new to me. Chastity and morality were praised and encouraged in my childhood. My introverted personality also buoyed me in that direction even when I was no longer under my mother's supervision. My determination to prove society wrong was in high gear. For twenty-three years, I had abstained from any sexual relationship. I had made the promise to God years back in my closet not to 'defile' myself with women in accordance with His Word; that is, my body being the temple of God. When I contemplated going to the seminary, it was to re-emphasize this promise.

I had studied God's covenant with Abraham in Genesis 17. I had also read Ecclesiastes 5:1-7 on issues concerning vows. I was aware of the consequences of reneging on a vow or otherwise: blessings for obedience and curses for disobedience. I knew I was dealing with a loving God who could at the same time be terrible or severe as described in Rom.11:22, Deut. 10:17, Neh. 1:8, Dan. 9:12 and the God who is a consuming fire in Deut. 4:24, Heb. 12:29; who visits the iniquities of fathers even to the third and fourth generations as told in Deut. 5:9-10. I knew I needed to tread carefully in order not to be on the wrong side of such a powerful God. To such a God, I had made a secret promise without anybody's promptings. Abstaining, therefore, was a forgone conclusion for me. Whether or not to abstain from sexual immorality was not the issue for me at that time. By the grace of God, the proposed covenant as it stood was something that was already secretly under implementation in my life. Making it formal in my pastor's presence felt like repeating a class to me. What was relevant to me at that time was knowing whether God would ever want me to marry or not. If yes, who? If not, how do I know? That was my genuine problem and that is where I needed spiritual help and guidance. I saw that period as an opportunity to enlist the help of my pastor on such a critical issue in my life, and I wanted it all done in secret in accordance with Matthew 6:6.

Another reason that prompted me to get out of the auditorium that evening was the legal wording of the covenant. It stipulated that we stay chaste, "until we entered the blessing of marriage." What, if one did not marry? What, if God did not want one to marry? Where was the person going to get the reward of such chastity from? Since the blessings from the exercise was legally tied to those who were going to marry, I felt it was unfair to those who may end up not marrying at all, and I feared that I could be one of them. I was aware God is an exact God. So, I needed to make sure I was asking for not only the right thing but specifically asking in the right way and wording. After listening to me, Pastor Boateng applauded my logic and zeal. He then encouraged me to communicate my demands to God the way I deemed fit while he took care of those inside. He left me alone, which I loved. It was better for people to assume I was opting out while in fact, I was still in it and was more advanced, than for them to be able to figure out exactly what was going on in my life. It was a secret between God and me, and I wanted it to remain as such.

"Commit thy way unto the Lord; trust also in Him; and He shall bring it to pass. And He shall bring forth thy righteousness as the light and thy judgment as the noonday." (Psalm 37:5-6 KJV)

As already indicated, sexual purity was not a problem for me. My problem was knowing what God had to say about it. Was I going to lose my virginity to marriage at some point in time? If so, to whom must I surrender this life-long cherished trophy? I needed answers to all these questions to make God's will perfect for my life. I remained quiet, gazing into the outer darkness that engulfed the surroundings that early night. Then I went into a period of meditation. With my eyes closed fixedly; my thoughts ran deep as I reflected on divine appointments. My mind first went to a deliverance session I had previously attended in which a demon was cast out. Upon his manifestation, the demon revealed that he managed to know and act deceitfully on the fellow because her conversation revealed her intentions and expectation. The demon, therefore, had to present a fake answer to the person to preempt God's will for that fellow. In Proverbs we also read, "Whoever guards his mouth preserves his life; he who opens wide his lips comes to ruin" (Prov. 13:3 ESV). This was enough warning for me to call for divine wisdom. With this background, I decided to communicate with God in my heart and spirit, and not utter a single word in the process. He who knew my heart knew my thoughts as well.

Ultimately, that precaution was not enough. Which part of His Word do I stand on? My thoughts switched to Judges 6. I had previously conducted an in-depth study of the book of Judges, so Gideon's story shot into my mind. Gideon asked for proofs from God three times to assure himself of the truth that God had truly chosen him to redeem Israel from Midianite oppression. The first proof occurred in verses 17–21 when he asked the angel, who was sent to deliver the message, to wait until he had brought him food:

> "The angel of God said to him, 'Place the meat and the unleavened bread on this rock, and pour the broth over it.' And Gideon did as he was told. Then the angel of the Lord touched the meat and bread with the tip of the staff in his hand, and fire flamed up from the rock and consumed all he had brought. And the angel of the Lord disappeared." (Judg. 6: 20–21 NLT)

That was the first proof. The message had been confirmed. The second and third proofs came when he was about to face the enemy. He had gathered his men but he still wanted to make assurance double sure. Here he goes again in verses 36–38:

> Then Gideon said to God, "If you are truly going to use me to rescue Israel as you promised, prove it to me in this way. I will put a wool fleece on the threshing floor tonight. If the fleece is wet with dew in the morning but the ground is dry, then I will know that you are going to help me rescue Israel as you promised." And that is just what happened. When Gideon got up early the next morning, he squeezed the fleece and wrung out a whole bowlful of water."(-Judg. 6:36–38 NLT)

If the second proof was an emphasis, Gideon wanted to put it beyond any shred of doubt in verses 39-40:

> Then Gideon said to God, "Please don't be angry with me, but let me make one more request. Let me

use the fleece for one more test. This time let the
fleece remain dry while the ground around it is wet
with dew." So that night God did as Gideon asked.
The fleece was dry in the morning, but the ground
was covered with dew."(Judg. 6:38–40 NLT)

Three times Gideon asked God for confirmation, and three times
God provided one. Gideon had no excuse anymore, so he had to
get to work.

Having thus reviewed the events in my mind, I concluded that if
God proved all of Gideon's demands and He was not dead but the
same living God, He should be able to prove my demands as well.
It should be that simple. "For whatsoever things were written afore-
time were written for our learning, that we through patience and comfort of the scriptures might have hope."(Rom. 15:4 KJV). So, me too,
I got to work where Gideon got going. I followed the same model to
petition God on my future life. I renewed my previous vows to God
and reiterated my determination to follow through to the end. I put
specific signs forward as my version of Gideon's tests. If indeed, "It
is not good for the man to be alone" (Gen. 2:18), He should confirm
specific signs to enable His son to know which way to go. I determined that if I do not see these signs by the time I hit middle age
(forty-five to fifty years of age), then that in itself constituted another
proof that He wanted me to stay a bachelor unto death, and I would
demand every single reward and blessing that accrued to chastity
in bachelorhood. The following were the demands I made on God:

SIGN #1

I prioritized a God-fearing woman in my request. If God was
willing that I marry, I wanted a woman who would complement my
godly principles and help me grow spiritually. I had come very far
with God, and as told in 1 Kings 11:1-4, the last thing I needed was

a wife who would turn my heart away from Him. Should that be the case, then I preferred not to marry at all. I did not know how this was going to unfold, but I expected to see total commitment and dedication to God on the part of my would-be wife. Her love for God and her thirst for righteousness must not be in question. Other than that, I needed no woman in my life.

SIGN #2

The next sign that came to my mind was perhaps the most audacious I sought from God. I reversed issues, which made it extremely difficult to fulfill, yet, as promised in Matthew 19:26, I expected the God of impossibility to act in fulfillment of His greatness. I wanted my would-be bride to make the proposal contrary to the prevailing culture. If this happened, it would be the clearest sign that such a woman was more likely to be my helper by divine appointment. The reason why this sign was important to me was that it was the most difficult to meet. I was born in a cultural setting where it was a taboo for a woman to propose to a man. There was the general notion that only whores would do so and nobody would want to marry a whore. Therefore, no woman in her right mind would do such a thing lest she ruin her possible future marriage. Any woman who ever did was deemed hopeless and up to no good. It was, therefore, impossible for women to propose. It was a tough demand, but I also understood that God was not human. He could cause that to happen if indeed He wanted to answer my request. I was very serious about that.

SIGN #3

The last idea that came to my mind was virginity. I leaned on Leviticus 21:13–15. I was not an ordained priest, yet I counted myself as one because I bore the name of a high priest. I had also come that far in my life and was still sexually unstained. It was, therefore, fair that I did not compromise on the same standards for my would-be wife. However, I was not sure how I was going to get a proof of this without intimacy, and I was not going to entertain such an idea prior to marriage either. Nevertheless, I had no doubt God was capable of getting me the message. It was His challenge not mine to worry about. After all, He was, is and will forever be omniscient.

I also placed great emphasis on virginity due to my hatred for cheating. If someone had been sleeping around while I was digging every spiritual nugget to keep my virginity intact, it would not be fitting to put a "new wine into an old skin." Our sexual joys must start together, at the same time, and at the same level. My wife could not be a professional in the act while I was still untested. I felt that such a situation may put a stress on both of us, especially on me, and create a tension in the marriage. We should all be novices at the time of marriage, so that we could learn and progress together.

After laying down these three requests, I took a very deep breath and sighed. Then I came out of my meditation. All these thoughts had happened without a single word. When I returned to the room to see the pastor, most of the youth who took the vow of chastity until marriage had left. Those who remained were those who wanted a counselor or to talk to the pastor. From then on, I lived in expectancy. If I did see all these signs in a lady, it would be the proof of His will for me to marry and to whom. I determined not to compromise on them or take a lenient approach. I put up three signs; therefore, I expected to see three signs. Even if one was missing in the person, I would not acquiesce. It should be either three of three or never. I was not worried at all by the difficulty of the demands. Even if I did not see them in any person and I hit middle age, that in itself was an answer to my quest. It would be His proof of bachelorhood for life. I had nothing to lose either way. My only duty then was to look forward to seeing those signs and guard against seduction. *Seduction*, that was my watchword.

PART II

CHAPTER 9

ENTRY OF SYLVIA

In 1977, when I had already started my elementary curriculum in a Local Authority school popularly known as Kuneso, something that would become significant in the future was unfolding about two hundred and twenty miles (350 km) away in a town called Winneba. It is an old town along the Atlantic coast of Ghana in the Gulf of Guinea. A significant number of its inhabitants are fisherfolk. It also has a considerable number of elite, highly educated citizens. The beaches attract a number of revelers to the town on a daily basis. However, the one thing that has attracted and still attracts the most people is its pagan festival called Aboakyer (Deer Hunting). A major highway connects the town to the nation's capital and to other major cities along the coastal stretch of Ghana. A number of schools, government institutions and agencies also promotes a sense of elitism in the town.

On the campus of the University College in the town lived Mr. and Mrs. Dadzie. Mr. Dadzie was a mathematics lecturer who resided in one of the university's chalets with his wife. On September 6, 1977, Mr. and Mrs. Dadzie had their second child. She was the couple's first and only daughter, a very tiny baby girl who weighed not more than four lbs (2kg). Apart from her hair which promised to

71

be unmanageable, everything else about her spelled the word *cute*. Quite unlike my own, her birth ignited ecstasy in the family. Mr. and Mrs. Dadzie named their baby girl Sylvia.

Like my parents, Mr. and Mrs. Dadzie were very religious. Mr. Dadzie was a man of principles, a mathematician and a lover of God. He made it his daily routine to teach the Bible to his family. Decades later, when I had the opportunity to visit them, he was still in the habit of having morning devotion with his family including his grandchildren. He would instruct them in a way that made it difficult for his children to hide their wrongdoings. He exemplified Abraham in Genesis, "I have singled him out so that he will direct his sons and their families to keep the way of the Lord by doing what is right and just. Then I will do for Abraham all that I have promised" (Gen. 18:19 NLT).

He loved his family and provided for them on a daily basis. He also took pleasure in teaching and nurturing students. He was neither rich nor flamboyant, but he managed his resources in a way that brought self-sufficiency to the family. Like Auntie Aggie, Mr. Dadzie was tough on discipline. He demanded good and godly behavior from his children at all times.

By the way, Auntie Aggie and Mrs. Dadzie (affectionately called Auntie Emma), bore a striking resemblance in many ways. For instance, the two figures had a similar physique, both tipping the scales and having thick arms. My mother was popularly called Auntie Aggie. In the same manner, Mrs. Dadzie was affectionately called Auntie Emma. Thus, both of them were everybody's Auntie in their respective communities.

Furthermore, they both took teaching appointments immediately after obtaining their Middle School Leaving Certificates (MLSC). While Auntie Aggie's teaching appointments once took her to a town called Ofoase in the Ashanti Region, Auntie Emma also taught in a town with a similar name, Akim-Ofoase in the Eastern Region. Moreover, they both later became bakers after leaving their teaching jobs, even though they baked different food products. Both of them even operated a provisions kiosk at one point in their lives to earn extra income to help their husbands. Sadly, each of them died in their mid-sixties; Auntie Aggie at sixty-five, Auntie Emma at sixty-six.

In contrast, Mrs. Dadzie was firm but less demanding in her manner with the children. Auntie Aggie had multiple engagements; hence she needed the children under her care to become independent as early as possible. This is what made her look stricter, sterner and more fearsome.

GROWING UP AND REDISCOVERY OF SELF

One might think that, as the only daughter in the family, Sylvia would enjoy special treatment from her parents. That turned out not to be the case. Mrs. Dadzie was rather strict on her, not wanting Sylvia to feel pompous. Mrs Dadzie looked at Sylvia in terms of the future when she would not be there for Sylvia. Sylvia's wrongs were more seriously condemned, and she was held to higher moral standards.

Furthermore, as a lecturer's daughter, Sylvia was under constant pressure to succeed academically. Even when a subject was hard for her to grasp, Mr. Dadzie would insist she mastered it if she ever dreamed of any peace of mind. Mr. Dadzie would sit her down and teach her till she pulled her weight. That meant less play and socialization for most of the time. As a child with an outgoing personality, this was a very disappointing outlook of life. Like many children under such circumstances, Sylvia's view about life was changing for the worse. Life was becoming all about adult bullying. There was a particular jealous woman in her extended family who viciously antagonized Sylvia even as a child. She envied the way Mr. and Mrs. Dadzie were molding their daughter and setting her up for future success while her own children had gone berserk. She constantly insulted Sylvia for no apparent reason. She would describe Sylvia in the most unprintable terms. This behavior on the part of an adult shook young Sylvia's confidence to the bottom. Eventually, Sylvia lost her self-esteem as this envious woman's negative comments sunk into her head.

During one vacation, Sylvia was invited by one of her uncles to spend the holidays with him at Tema, a town very close to the capital. During this period, something happened that changed Sylvia's perception about her own self. She was alone at her uncle's home as the entire household had gone to work. She stood in front of a big mirror and looked at her full body after shower. She was struck by what she saw. Sylvia looked at her growing feminine body features and observed her developing curves. She was surprised at how beautiful she was. She was so pleased with herself that she could not help but exclaim to herself, "Wow! What a beautiful girl I am!" Sylvia realized she was not as undesirable as she had been made to think of herself in the past. That was when she rediscovered her self-esteem. This period marked her entry into true individuality. She realized she needed no one's compliment to feel fulfilled. She would not be bothered by adverse negative statements about her either. Like myself, she came to believe she was a complete whole and had a stable personality in herself regardless of other people's views about her.

CHARTING A COURSE FOR LIFE

> *"Thy word is a lamp unto my feet and a light*
> *unto my path."*
> —Psalms 119:105 (KJV)

Due to her parents' love for God, Sylvia and her siblings frequented the services and the programs in between every Sunday at the chapel. That is when Sylvia learned lessons about righteousness. Children's Bible studies were a must. In addition, Mr. Dadzie instituted early morning devotional sessions for the entire family. At 5

A.M., he would get up and wake every member of the family for prayer and biblical exhortations. He would lead the family in a short Bible study, elicit lessons for living therefrom and encourage everybody to emulate the good principles and eschew the bad examples. During the session, any child who had been caught in any adverse behavior prior to morning devotions would be seriously chastised, counseled and admonished. In fact, offending children were made to feel very guilty. Thereafter, they would be made to confess their wrongdoing before the gathered members of the family. There was no threat of the cane as there was at the Co-operative House, yet no child could hide his or her wrongs.

In the end, the family would pray together to begin the day. That was how a typical day began for Sylvia. Right from the beginning, morality and godliness were projected before her eyes as prized values worth living for and that became the perspective from which she looked at everything. The stage was thus set for her future course of life.

Sylvia grew up to be a very disciplined girl with a lot of respect for the elderly, her teachers and her peers. She loved both her parents very much but was more attached to her father. Later, the family moved to a family house in the eastern part of Winneba as her father had to leave for a course in Kumasi. Mr. Dadzie had gained admission to the Kwame Nkrumah University of Science and Technology to pursue a further course of study in Mathematics.

Upon enrollment, Mr Dadzie took a teaching job in Technology High School as a Mathematics tutor. This enabled him to still provide for his family while studying at the same time. Even with a reduced income as he downgraded from lecturer to tutor, he still managed to put up a three-bedroom apartment for his family on his wife's family land. This insulated his family from other family member's intrusion into their lives. Mr. Dadzie was respectful and decent; hence he did not want any friction between his family and other members of their extended family.

As fate would have it, Mr Dadzie was to spend more years in Kumasi than he originally anticipated. He tried to visit his family at regular intervals. During vacations, he would leave Kumasi for Winneba and spend virtually the entire holiday period with his family. There were times that the family visited him but that was very rare. When his research work would not allow him to travel, Sylvia, would pay him a visit and spend some of her vacation time with him, cooking and doing the laundry for him.

In 1991, Sylvia gained admission into the Wesley Girls' High School, then the most elite girls' school in Ghana. Even though Mr. Dadzie did not have much money, he managed to see her through to high school. At the age of fourteen, with her father in Kumasi and mother in Winneba, Sylvia left for Cape Coast, a distance of about fifty-five miles (88km) from Winneba to begin her high school life.

Life in high school was a bit tough as Sylvia felt quite separated from her loving parents, especially from her father who was challenged by distance and time. If Mr. Dadzie was not studying, he was working and hardly had time to make the journey from Kumasi to the Cape Coast to visit his daughter. Mrs. Dadzie, however, managed to squeeze some time off her schedule to visit Sylvia a couple of times before the academic term ended most of the time. Sylvia's academic studies were also very challenging as she had to rub shoulders with the cream of the crop. As an elite school, Wesley Girls' High School attracted a large portion of the most brilliant students. Therefore, Sylvia had to keep her academic wheels spinning all the time in order to keep pace with the competition. She studied very hard and aimed higher.

Dutiful as she was trained to be, Sylvia never shied away from even more duty and responsibility. She put this character she had developed on full display during her academic life at Wesley Girls' High School. She got involved in extra-curricular activities and other responsibilities. Despite the academic challenge, Sylvia joined the school's athletic team as a sprinter. She ran the 100m event and the

4×100m relay. Her tiny body, slim legs, and lightweight naturally made her agile enough for running, and she did not find it difficult gaining a position on the team. After just a few weeks of trial training, she was in for good. Sylvia especially loved the inter-collegiate athletic competitions in which her school competed with other schools in the region. She eventually became the prefect of her class. She was also designated a Dormitory Monitor, a position that made her responsible for her peers' punctuality in wake-up times, evening devotion and observation of Lights Out time in the dormitory.

In all these growing responsibilities, Sylvia never forgot God. She stayed faithful and kept her Bible close. There were instances in which she was penalized at prep time in the evening when she was found reading the Bible instead of her school notes, but this did not douse her spirit as she continued to study the Bible during most of her free time and before she began studying her class notes at prep times. There were many things in the Bible that Sylvia did not understand yet like me, that did not in any way affect her obsession with the Bible. She believed that the Bible, as the Word of God, held the secret to life and its sanctity was never in doubt. She sometimes went off campus on exeat to visit local churches for outreach programs. She was exceptionally motivated by the desire and the possibility of seeing God as expressed in Hebrews, "Make every effort to live in peace with all men and to be holy; without holiness, no one will see the Lord." (Heb.12:14 NIV). Sylvia measured her life with these virtues and always tried to live up to them. Her enthusiasm was boosted by her thinking that she could see God if she became as holy as God. All she wanted to do was to live a life of godliness in the hope of seeing God face-to-face. Though she did not understand the fact that the only way God chose to reveal Himself in human form was through the Lord Jesus Christ, Sylvia's efforts toward godliness left a lasting trait of virtue in her.

LOVE FOR GOD CAME NATURALLY

"You are not what others think you are. You are what
God knows you are."
—Shannon Alder

Sylvia became a sweet, innocent and outgoing girl. Being kind to others and helping the vulnerable in society was something she grew to love. She loved to talk to people and to listen to them. She became more interested in missionary work as her views about marriage evolved. Increasingly, she became even more devoted to the work of God. Sylvia would take active part in her church's visits to the prisons and collection of donations to the vulnerable in society. She would give her clothing and savings for charity. She took an active part in evangelism. The more she grew, the more Sylvia love for God's work increased. In her teenage years, she read the Bible extensively, and she would pray and fast often to nourish her spirit. She would sometimes take her Bible and embark on the work of evangelism on her own, going from street to street and from house to house telling both old and young about the saving work of Jesus Christ on the cross. Her parents' admonishing and constant scripture reading made Sylvia choose godliness and morality over the pleasures and pressures of immoral and sinful lives. She abhorred her fellow friends who gave themselves to men immorally. She detested seeing pregnant girls without marriage vows or marriage rings on their fingers. The problems that some of her peers went through as a result of fornication, coupled with the strict moral standards established by her parents, made Sylvia a staunch advocate of sexual purity.

Sylvia became more and more disposed toward a life of pure celibacy. Although she did not take a vow as I did, she saw no other way to please God, her parents and herself other than through abstinence. Living a life sexually unstained was something Sylvia cherished and wanted to achieve. She considered the achievement of this goal as very important in life. At a certain point in time, as chastity became an uncontrollable force in her life, Sylvia could not really tell if she would marry. She advocated godliness and sexless celibacy for all young people. She was happy to serve the Lord even if it meant her giving up marrying in future. In fact, it wasn't until later in life when God miraculously hit her with Cupid's arrow, that she ever entertained any idea of marriage.

By the middle of 1994, Sylvia had completed high school and was contemplating whether to go to the university or to a technical college to learn a trade. Her older brother had also completed senior high school around the same time. Sylvia had actually caught up with her elder brother in their elementary school days because she was accelerated into the next class level due to her academic prowess. Mr. Dadzie now had two post-high school children to care for as the last born was also in the making. This was financially burdensome for a man who was also undertaking further studies,. Therefore, Mr Dadzie encouraged Sylvia and her brother to take the vocational option as that came with lesser costs. He encouraged his daughter to enter into a Teacher Training College to learn the teaching profession while he sent his son to a Polytechnic school. That was the best idea at that time because the government of Ghana gave monthly allowances to students in Teacher Training Colleges to help them pay for their academic expenses. This would be a huge relief for Mr. Dadzie as it would cut costs for him. So, in 1995, he bought application forms for his daughter.

In early October of that year, Sylvia was invited to take the entrance examination and have an interview. Mr. Dadzie put all his priorities aside and accompanied his daughter to the entrance examination at Mount Mary Teacher Training College. Fortunately for them, they met one of the students Mr Dadzie had taught in the University College years ago. She was a Mathematics tutor in this particular Training College. As a respected lecturer in Mathematics,

Mr. Dadzie received a considerable measure of hospitality from this particular tutor. She accommodated both father and daughter, and fed them for the three days that they spent on the campus. On the third day, when the results were announced, Sylvia had passed and gained admission to the college. She was to return to start the course within two weeks. Mr. Dadzie could not hide his joy. His daughter would be a teacher in the French language and become financially independent.

Sylvia's independence would be a huge lift from his shoulders. Mr. Dadzie could not fathom how he was going to foot the expanding bills of his family with a static and predictable income like his in the future. Life was becoming really tough. For now, Mr Dadzie could at least hope that Sylvia's independence was on the horizon. Very soon, he would be able to spread his meager salary on other evolving issues in the family. Mr. Dadzie was able to provide Sylvia's basic needs for college and got her ready. On the day of her departure, both Mr. and Mrs. Dadzie sat Sylvia down and took turns advising her on the need to study hard. As usual, they also stressed spirituality. They prayed for her after which Mrs. Dadzie accompanied Sylvia to the bus terminal where she saw her daughter off to college. Sylvia was not so overwhelmed at leaving home again because she had already experienced boarding house in high school where, she had gained the necessary self-confidence and independence to be on her own.

Moreover, this event marked Sylvia's journey into adulthood and full independence, which was something she looked forward to. Having said goodbye to her parents, Sylvia departed to Mount Mary College to begin her career in teaching. She arrived on the college campus in the evening of October 6, 1995, a week before the official arrival time for many new students. Sylvia's father intentionally sent her off in advance of the reopening date to allow her to gain knowledge of the campus and familiarize herself with the new environment before official classes began. Young as she still was, Sylvia was prepared and independent enough to start college life.

PART III

CHAPTER 10

ARRIVAL ON COLLEGE CAMPUS

"A man's heart plans his way: but the Lord directs his steps."
—Proverbs 16:9 (NKJV)

By June 1995, those of my "A" Level colleagues who passed the first sitting had completed their bachelor's degree courses with full honors. Some secured permanent employment while others who wanted to go up still were pursuing their master's degrees. Most of the latter were Teaching Assistants in their respective universities. Meanwhile, I was stuck in a poor-paying job at a private elementary school owned by a family. All the non-teaching staff were family members, some of whom could not make a single sentence in the English language without a grammatical accident. Apart from the head teacher, none of the office staff had any plausible academic certificate to their credit. Yet these were the people I was subordinated to. *Was that all the brilliance in me deserved?* I asked myself. People who were not my match academically were lording it over me in that place of employment. This pushed me to act out the "dog going back to its vomit" routine. I reconsidered

83

enrolling in one of the Teacher Training Colleges, an idea I had previously rejected vehemently. At least, I would be respected as a professional teacher. I was teaching anyway, so what prevented me from professionalizing it? This time I bought the application forms myself, filled it out and sent it in. I went for the entrance and placement examination, which looked like a practice test for me. After three days of oral and written tests coupled with interviews, I passed and was given a spot in Mount Mary College to become a teacher in the French language. I was asked to return in two weeks' time to start the course. Was that the end of the wilderness? We will see.

I still did not like the idea of becoming a teacher. Teaching is certainly not the job for an introvert. While some people cried over not making the list, I looked on with indifference. On my way back to Kumasi from the College campus at Somanya, I confided in some newfound friends who were on the bus with me, and who also took part in the entrance exam, that I may not show up for the course. I was uncertain about pursuing a teacher training course, so I kept the offer to myself until Azay asked me about it. While he was happy for me for the offer, I was not happy for myself. I had no excuse either, so I made the decision to accept the offer of admission and show up—at least to see what would happen. I made up my mind only four days before the start of the first trimester. My preparation was somewhat haphazard. I did not look like someone who was going away for months as I set off to Mount Mary College campus with a few provisional items. It was a journey of about one hundred and forty-three miles (two hundred and thirty kilometers) from home. I arrived in the evening of October 12, 1995 to another boarding house experience. In-processing was quick, and I passed my first night peacefully. The next day we were shown our respective classrooms where I picked a right-angled spot created by the first column of desks and the very last row. I sat with my back to one wall and another to my left. I chose that spot for a purpose. As an introvert, I did not like it when people watched me from behind. That spot offered me a sense of security. Everybody else sat either in front of me or to my right.

Two weeks into the trimester, I still could not really bring myself to settle in. The prevailing atmosphere at the college drove me crazy. I hatched a plan to go AWOL. I planned to leave campus while classes were in session to avoid being seen. I was waiting for the most opportune time when suddenly the news came in that a mate of ours had already taken the wind out of my sails. He vanished from campus and was being sought after. Security alertness was heightened while everybody else and the authorities were on the watch. I realized that I was not the only person at the college who was not happy with himself. This encouraged my idea to bolt but the heightened security prevented me from making any move — at least not that very moment.

Nonetheless, I kept planning secretly and weighing my options. Then, when everything seemed set for me to carry out my version of the vanishing act, I got a surprise visit from my father. He was on his way to Accra, the nation's capital. He asked me how I was faring but I could not muster the courage to reveal my plans to him. The last thing I wanted was to make my plans known to anybody. So, I answered that everything was well with me. After he had left, I regretted because my cover-up left no excuse for me to return home. What would Azay say if I did pop up in his house all of a sudden? How was I going to defend my return? He really believed in my academic ability and was happy for me upon my admission. I could not imagine dashing his hope and belief in me. Facing the reality of abandoning my studies was becoming too complicated for me, so I shelved the idea for the moment. Life continued as usual on campus. Initially, classes were boring because the presentation of materials was below my standard. I was cut out for the university, I felt. Therefore, any intermediary course felt like too much repetition for me. My only motivation was the high marks I was scoring in class. I also took to the library to get ahead. I intentionally sacrificed some lectures for the library where I could research more into the French language to give myself an advantage in the course. If I went to class, I would walk straight past everybody into my corner, hardly talking to anyone. Things went on like this until about five weeks into the trimester when something happened that put me in my longest challenge yet.

The French Club on campus staged a drama one Saturday evening which was designated for such entertainment. However, I was more interested in a book I was reading than the drama. I kept my head down reading. In one of the scenes on stage I heard a lady's voice piercing the hall in fluent and impeccable French with a sweet-sounding accent. That sweet voice blew my mind completely away. When I threw my book onto my lap and stretched my neck to catch a glimpse of who this cute lady was, I realized I was not the only one. All heads were up and eyes were fixed upon the stage. The impressive French vibrating from a melodious voice on the stage held the audience captive. I said to myself, *That is the kind of French I would like to speak.*

But who was this lady? I would never know until five days after the drama when I learned her name was Sylvia Dadzie. She was in my class, and she was even appointed the Assistant Class Prefect. I hardly knew her and had not yet spoken to her. More than a month after my arrival on campus, I had not spoken to the majority of my mates especially the ladies and I did not care either. I was particularly mindful of my vows and would not in any way put myself in a situation where I could be endangered. *Could she possibly be my future wife?* I dreamed for a while, but I promptly dismissed such a fantasy from my mind. That was never going to happen because of three reasons. First, she looked too expensive in the drama which was something that I was not prepared to risk my future bank account on. Second, I was not among the handsome guys who could even catch the eyes of such a beautiful lady let alone become her guy. Third, she came from an ethnic group whose ladies my mother detested. Their ladies were reputed to be spendthrifts and fashion hungry. My mother would have no such woman for her son. I could, therefore, not even think of befriending her let alone suggest a relationship. I noticed her for the first time but kept my distance as with any other lady on campus.

Meanwhile, I kicked my godly life up a notch. Luckily, there was a Scripture Union group on this campus too; I did not hesitate to join it and became a very active member. Somehow, Sylvia had noticed my diligence with this group as well as my brilliance in class. Questions that seemed very difficult to her, I answered with fluidity and comprehension. As the Assistant Prefect for our class, she recorded our class performance for the tutors and had noticed my exceptionally high scores. Coincidentally, she was naturally attracted to brilliant men. Ironically, while I had secretly written off any possibility of friendship with her, Sylvia, on the other hand, was secretly contemplating, *This is the kind of guy worth befriending*. These two contrasting positions played out interestingly in our subsequent interactions. The bottom line for me was not simple at all. I was hopeful but fearful at the same time. Nothing is as disturbing as hope tinged with fear. I was hopeful because I was expecting God to communicate His will to me as to whether He wanted me to marry or not. If positive, I was going to know who it was. On the other hand, I feared this because such an expectation made me susceptible to seduction or deception. The only way I could violate my covenant with God was through seduction by a lady into commission of fornication. Furthermore, the only way I could be seduced was to get closer to or listen to women. That was my mentality for that moment at least. Other than that, I saw no way I could be tempted to violate my vows, and I knew the evil consequences should I break them. That personal commitment to chastity rendered me very hard on the opposite sex. I was not nice at all to ladies because I saw them as extremely risky to my celibacy vow.

I tended to see every lady as a possible obstacle more than as an accessory to my blessing. I would rather not know the will of God for me than to become a victim in the process.

Sylvia was taken ill in the last third of the trimester, and she was admitted in one of the nearby hospitals. That was when I got to know just how popular she was. The entire campus was filled with news about her. Everybody talked fondly about her. Tiny, cute, beautiful, friendly, kind and respectful were the most frequently occurring adjectives I heard from other students and tutors' descriptions of her. Almost the entire campus visited Sylvia at the hospital at one time or another. There were days that the number of well-wishers were cut short by college authorities because they were too many. However, I made no such attempt.

A week after Sylvia was admitted to the hospital, she was discharged and came back to campus. Many people sought to welcome her back to campus upon her arrival. Once again, I was absent from such endeavors. After lunch that day, some mates of ours came to me and told me that Sylvia was in the classroom, and they were going to welcome her back. I thought it a good idea, so I joined them. Sylvia was all smiles until it came to my turn when she expressed her disappointment: She had expected to see me among the visitors who came to the hospital but I never showed up. I did not understand that and I was quite upset. *Why was she expecting me there? Why was she thinking about me? What was so special about me that made me automatically responsible for her? Did I come here to study or to visit patients? Was she sent by the devil to torment me?* These were some of the questions that were running through my mind. I left her immediately and returned to my dormitory still fuming with Sylvia's reaction. I folded up and recoiled completely within after that. I avoided her as much as I could and did not talk to her. This went on until the end of the trimester when we were dismissed for the Christmas holidays, which was quite a relief for me. For the next few weeks I would not have to deal with her.

After the holidays, we returned to campus to continue our academic studies. I still kept my distance from Sylvia as with any other lady and wished I were in a different class. While she did not know I was upset about what happened the previous trimester, it was still fresh in my mind. Once she came to my desk and asked me if there was anything wrong with me. By my queer behavior she deduced that I might be a miserable fellow. As compassionate as she was, she was moved to seek my welfare. I replied in the negative but still distanced myself from her. I had already concluded that friendship or relationship with her was impossible, so I was not in any hurry to restore normalcy in our interactions or appease anybody who had been upset with me previously. I was also equally upset, so what was the big deal? In spite of her efforts to smile at me, I would not reciprocate and avoided her. In fact, I was so cold toward her that Sylvia got tired of this behavior of mine and stopped trying to get me to come around. For a while, we completely relapsed and for weeks on end we would not talk to each other even though we were in the same class. In order to avoid meeting her at all, I would quickly run back to the classroom at each break and take my seat before anybody else did. If not, I would walk in late when everybody was already seated, sometimes with lectures in progress. In this manner, I deprived everybody, especially Sylvia of the chance to meet let alone talk to me.

Notwithstanding this seemingly self-induced blackout, I noticed something during the period. Anytime I entered the class late, I walked past everybody, head bowed, to take my seat. Often, when I turned to sit, my eyes met Sylvia's gaze. This girl was surely stealing glances at me but that meant nothing to me because I had completely ruled her out of my life. Quite unknown to me, she had begun investigating me quietly and earnestly. She realized I talked freely and laughed heartily around Vincent, who sat in front of me and with whom I had many things in common. Yet with everybody else, I kept a very serious, straight and unwelcoming face. I talked very little and reduced every question to a yes or no response.

With such a cryptic life, Sylvia concluded that I might be hiding something. This made her all the more curious about me, and she wanted to know more. *Why do most brilliant people tend to be quiet and nonchalant?*, she wondered. She wanted to find out more about me, but my non-communicative stance was giving her a hard time. She did not want to appear intrusive either. Therefore, she considered collecting information about me informally. Here too, she did not make any progress as I was as mysterious to everybody else as I was to her. Consequently, she resorted to making anecdotes about me through strict observation. Anytime a very challenging question was thrown at the class that reduced everybody to head-scratching, Sylvia would look expectantly all the way back at my direction from her seat in the front row as if to say, *Come on, boy! I know you can do it*. And when I answered correctly, I could see some brightness ignite in her face. That was significant, but as green and pessimistic as I was with ladies, especially with Sylvia, I did not make any meaning out of that. What I cherished though was that, after so many years in the wilderness, it was refreshing to again see that somebody still believed in my academic ability.

Later, in that same trimester, there was an athletic competition between the various housing divisions on campus. I did not know Sylvia was a runner until I saw her run the sprints for her house. That got me back up because Track was and still is one of my favorite sports. She always looked like the smallest runner in any line up. However, with her tiny limbs and slim body, nimbleness was a given. If the wind blew in the same direction of her travel, her feet hardly touched the ground. She earned my admiration, but I would never express it to her or even publicly for fear of being misinterpreted. In one of the 100-meter race events, she tripped and fell. When I saw the First Aid team bring her to the shade where

I was for treatment, I left the place immediately to avoid having to talk to her. However, I saw her in the classroom during prep hours that evening, and felt obliged to show sympathy. I hesitated as a mental argument ensued in my head. I finally dropped my antagonistic posture and asked if she got hurt. This time I would not be left out—once bitten, twice shy. She explained to me that she sustained a few bruises, but she was ready to run the next day. That got us back onto talking terms, but not as fluid. Occasionally, Sylvia would bring up a topic or a lesson she had little understanding for us to discuss. Even so, I remained largely distant and less communicative until the next trimester when events developed more rapidly.

Chapter 11

Unique Partnerships

The Duo

Can two walk together, unless they have agreed to do so? —Amos 3:3 (NIV)

The following trimester was the most dramatic for me. There was going to be student elections on campus to replace the outgoing student government for the coming academic year. A day was set aside for candidates to present their manifestoes to the student body. There would not be any classes that morning to allow candidates to prepare to face the student body in a forum. I was not going to waste the morning. Knowing the classroom would be quiet that period, I went there to study before the activities started.

Surprisingly, Sylvia also had the same idea and popped up after I had been there for about forty minutes. She walked straight to me and sat right next to me. *This girl again! How did she know I was here and what does she want from me?* I wondered. I felt very uncomfortable. She had already observed my diligence not only in class but in the programs of the Scripture Union on campus as well. She was curious about my zeal for Christ and what made

93

me academically so bright when, in fact, my inter-personal relationships were so poor. She had also noticed that I had taken an entrenched shy position that made me almost impossible to befriend. She wondered if I was pretending or if I was genuinely shy. In order to get me to open up, she adopted a common grounds approach. She was tiny, but she had a lot of wits in her. Knowing my interest in the Bible, she brought up a scripture passage that attracted my attention. Once I began to respond, she gradually deviated. The scripture discussion then degenerated into personal affairs. She asked me several questions that touched on my upbringing and personal life.

Initially, I was not forthcoming because I was afraid that she might seduce me. Anytime I encountered a lady, I remembered my vows and I saw proceedings through that lens. I would not prolong any conversation with a lady whenever I had one. Sylvia realized that I was uncomfortable. My responses to her were becoming shorter and crispier. To get me to talk to her candidly, she varied her strategy. By this time, she had left my side and taken a seat in the opposite direction such that we were now looking at each other face-to-face still, but from a distance with a table between us. That gave me a breathing space so I balanced myself in my chair. She then self-disclosed, telling me more about herself and the fact that she also loved God the way I did. I found a common ground in that statement which encouraged me to open up again. We went back to the Bible every now and then in our conversation.

When she realized that I was again relapsing into short, crisp sentences, Sylvia varied her strategy again. It was a battle of wits. She mentioned that she had been to Kumasi several times and shared with me where her father stayed. Then, she asked if I knew that suburb. Of course, I knew the place, so she got me talking. She finally got me to reveal my full identity, and I told her some of the challenges I had experienced growing up especially my journey with Christ and my views about the world. She realized that when it came to Christ Jesus, the Word of God, and godly living, we had so much in common. During our discourse, our statements were interwoven with biblical references and inferences. Sylvia gradually took over the conversation and talked more intimately with me. She told me about how her friendliness was misinterpreted by some gentlemen such that they made undesirable advances toward her. However, she abhorred such behaviors and would not engage in any such illicit relationships. I was not comfortable talking about such issues since I was afraid it might take us onto what I considered a slippery slope, and I was not ready for that. I did not want to seem rude to her either, so I resorted to non-verbal cues. I stated my objection to her conversation by sitting back and gazing strictly into my book. In my head I was asking, *Which direction is this lady going? Will she stop before I get out of the room?* However, she got my antennae raised when she confessed that she had been watching me and had seen me to be decent, humble, and God fearing. "I can see you are academically very bright, but you never boast about it. Also, every evening after supper, I see you walk to the field to pray. Many Scripture Union members say you never miss any of their meetings, but you hardly ever talk. I understand they only hear your voice during Bible Study sessions. Is that true?" she enquired. I smiled and turned my head slightly leftwards and away from her but did not answer. She interpreted that to mean affirmation so she continued, "To me, that is very remarkable. I would appreciate it if we could be friends and study partners so that we can help each other," she concluded. I was completely taken aback, and she saw both surprise and rebuttal on my face. In my head I was saying, *This is it! I have found the devil. She is here to seduce me.* Realizing that I was not comfortable with the idea, Sylvia quickly emphasized that she meant this to be purely platonic and for academic purposes; no personal relationship intended. I heaved a sigh of relief within me but I still remained silent, looking down at the table between us. I was conducting a mental assessment of the threat. She got up and asked if I found her suggestion uncomfortable. Obviously, it was, but for the assurance she gave me and the genuineness of her heart, I could not reject her idea outright. It took me some time to arrive at a positive answer for her. She spoke with sincerity and frankness, an attribute that convinced me beyond doubt. Nevertheless, I reminded her that if she meant us to be just friends and for the sake of our studies, she should respect her word, citing Thessalonians:

> "God's will is for you to be holy, so stay away from
> all sexual sin. Then each of you will control his own
> body and live in holiness and honor—not in lustful
> passion like the pagans who do not know God and
> His ways." (1 Thess. 4:3-5 NLT)

I gathered the courage to emphasize to Sylvia that she should consider the friendship over and the study partnership abrogated if she even winked an eye at me once. I said this in reference to my vows, but I did not tell her about it. This was still an unspoken secret between God and I. I still believed there was no way she could end up being the woman in my covenant. That encouraged me to lower the barrier with her. I entertained a little fear, regardless. I was very wide awake watching out: any sign of deviation from the original intent of the friendship and it would be over. I would flee in accordance with the epistle to Timothy: "Flee also youthful lusts: but follow righteousness, faith, charity, peace, with them that call on the Lord out of a pure heart." (2 Tim. 2:22 KJV).

Sylvia was purely motivated to seek partnership and friendship with me because she had observed that I almost always scored higher marks than our classmates. She knew that I would definitely be very helpful as academic study partner. Moreover, she hoped that my godly stance, non-talkative demeanor, and uncompromising character would keep other men away from approaching her with immoral requests if they knew I was her close friend and study partner. She was right as we saw later. Sometimes I marveled at how she solved her own problem with my reputation or other people's input. I wished I were that savvy.

On the other hand, Sylvia might be able to help me relate better with other students on campus. Finally, and more importantly to her, she might be able to find out the truth underlying my mysterious behavior, a quest which she never succeeded until ten years later. But, talk about a pure, sincere heart, and I would point out to you a lady who had one. After our conversation and self-disclosures, it was time for the student politics forum to begin. We left the classroom and headed toward the assembly grounds. For the first time in over twenty years of my life, I held the hand of a lady who was neither my mother nor my sister. I had never felt so comfortable with a lady as I did on that day. I could see her clothed in pure heartedness and heard the gladness in her voice. I was very convinced she was godly, innocent, and decently tongued.

Despite her popularity on campus, Sylvia was very humble, wise, graceful, sympathetic, very thoughtful and academically hungry. She sometimes complained about the attention she was getting on campus. However, I saw it as natural. As tiny and cute as she was, other students and officials could not help interacting with her at the least chance. In most of our subsequent encounters, we would pray before any discussion took place. That gesture cemented my trust in her and erased any fear I had with her. In our final year in college, I knew I could trust her absolutely as I trusted myself.

The forum had already taken shape when we got there. We stood together at the back observing and listening to what the candidates had to offer. After the forum, we headed back to the classroom. On the way we talked about which of the candidates was worthy of our votes. Her top picks coincided with mine. Surprisingly, we seemed to reason alike; it was strictly along godly and moral lines.

Ironically, she would be a candidate vying for the Ladies' Sports Prefect position in a similar forum in the following academic year. We would discuss her plans and her program for the position, and I would draft her manifesto speech. She would go on to become the Sports Prefect with a majority vote but at this point, none of us had the slightest idea about such a future.

Back in the classroom, we considered the modalities upon which our proposed friendship and study partnership would be based. Just before we broke for lunch, we made a schedule for the various subjects that needed extra effort to master. These included mainly French subjects, especially in the areas of grammar and phonetics. Later on, we updated the schedule to include very early morning on weekends to accommodate the extensive reading needed for English and French literature. It was a very good plan for us as it put a lot of pressure on us to study. For instance, the modalities stipulated that we read and researched in advance, if needed, to gain some mastery in at least certain parts of the subjects before we met for discussion. Neither of us wanted to disgrace him- or herself by having nothing to contribute during discussion. So, we constantly burned the midnight oil.

Whenever the task involved both extensive reading and research, we would divide it among ourselves. I usually opted to do the harder part—the research—because I was more advanced in my studies. However, Sylvia saw this in a different way. She felt that my choosing to do the harder part of the tasks was a sign of sympathy on my part as though, I was willing to go the extra mile just to make things easier on my partner. Down within her, she wanted to commend me for such conduct and to encourage me to take it into marriage if I ever would. Nonetheless, knowing how negative I was to relationship matters she was careful not to say or do anything that would jeopardize the foundation of our friendship. She kept it to herself. While I would leave her to go to the library for research, Sylvia would do the reading and identify sticky points that needed further elaboration. Any time we met for discussion, it was a very busy affair. We would rack our brains a lot in those times yet neither of us would concede tiredness even if we were. It turned out to be a very useful exercise for us. We deepened our knowledge as we had the opportunity to teach and explain things to each other. We also got to know each other's strengths even more. I benefited especially as my shyness with women gradually dissipated as the trimesters passed. Eventually, I was able to talk confidently with other women on campus.

I never compromised on my worship. Even though Sylvia occasionally attended the Scripture Union programs, her attendance became more frequent when we started studying together. I also visited her church meetings on campus but only twice. I had a position of leadership in the Scripture Union, so I always had a role to play and I could not afford to be absent myself. We very much liked the principles upon which we had based our friendship. We conducted ourselves so decently and morally that both of us did not have any reason to doubt each other. The trimester went by very quickly.

During vacation, Sylvia and I corresponded with each other through the postal service. Still, our correspondence was godly and morally uplifting. We mostly shared lessons we had learned from the Bible in each other's absence. We also shared our exceptional experiences that were worth telling. One characteristic of our correspondence was that at the tail end of it, we would always encourage each other to stay strong and pure for God. The admonishment would end with well wishes and a short prayer. This became the trend every vacation, even after we completed college.

Sylvia and I at the College Library.

THE TSEINOOS

*"Excellence is the gradual result of always striving
to do better."*
—Pat Riley

Less than three weeks after we had cemented our partnership, there arose an occasion when the class had to be divided into groups for academic purposes especially in the Oral French aspects. The class Prefects were tasked with this assignment. When the list was displayed on the notice board for every class member to locate his or her group, I found myself in Sylvia's group. I began to open my eyes. I knew I did not end up in her group by accident. Mind you, as the Assistant Class Prefect who was rather more active than the substantive prefect, Sylvia had a hand in determining who went to which group. Initially, I was a bit concerned about conflict of interest issues. However, the list had already been approved by the class tutor, so I took it easy.

There were other three gentlemen in the group, namely; Vincent, Gideon, and Charles. Sylvia and Sitsofe were the only ladies. When we had fulfilled the purposes for which the groups were established, they were disbanded by the authorities. However, given the tremendous impact of individual contributions on our group objectives, we voluntarily chose to maintain our group, redefine our group objectives, and extend our group activities to cover all other subjects. We changed its official name from "Group 5" to the "Agooji Group." Later, it became popularly known as the "Koo Group" because of the way we referred to ourselves in public which originally stemmed from a joke Vincent told. We usually called one another "*Koo*," a local term for bosom friend. That showed the kind of affection we had for one another. Of course, it was always a happy group. As the trimester dragged on, our group's discussions became more interesting and unique. We got to know ourselves more and helped one another academically. Socially, we established closer bonds with one another. We worked as a team and stuck together like a family.

Each one of us had a unique talent, which also made the group unique. I was the typical task-oriented member of the group who usually dropped the academic load on the shoulders of the group to handle. Sometimes, I would go to the library to do more research on certain topics especially on French grammar and phonetics. Whatever I discovered, I would bring my notes to the group for us to discuss further and share the notes. The rest would, in turn, brief me on lessons they'd had while I was away at the library.

Vincent, on the other hand, was the 'comedian' in the group. He focused on interspersing our discussions with humorous stories and interjections. He made sure the group never got bored. His funniness sometimes threw the group into wild laughter for minutes.

Sometimes, we laughed so loud that other students would come out of their study rooms to see what was happening. In one of his humorous stories, the term *Tseinoo* was invented. Subsequently, that word became the final name of the group as we tended to use that term more than the "Koo" during the final days.

Sitsofe, a serious, decent, and respectful lady with a beautiful nose was the time keeper and guardian of the group's objectives. She was the most determined in the group. Whenever we drifted off course, she would step in and remind us of our objectives and the time within which they must be achieved. She would draw us out of laughter and deviation back to the discussion forum to make sure we stayed on course and finished on time. She was soft-spoken with an attractive, slightly gap-toothed smile but was very determined. She was not noted for athletics as Sylvia was but with such a great determination she could be anything. One day, she gave us a dose of such determination during athletics competition with other colleges in the region. Our college was in short supply of track athletes. Sitsofe stepped up to the plate and did not disappoint at all. She was the anchorwoman for our college women's athletic team in a 4×400 meter relay race. She took the baton from a teammate at a miserable third position. With more than eighty meters between her and the lady in the first position, she gave a hot chase, ignoring the lady in her immediate front and fixing her eyes continuously on the one in the lead. As if she was possessed, this lady constantly paced wider and faster until she caught up with the lady in the first position and overtook her with about seven meters to the tape. Everybody was astonished. Indeed, she made our college proud and her fame spread on campus. Even prouder was the Tseinoo Group when we realized we were not only good in academics but had excellent athletic heroines in our midst as well.

Gideon, a skinny gentleman with a relatively small head was the gesturing man in the group. Before a word came out of his mouth, he would gesture it five times. He would never talk with his hands down, which in a way also made him an interesting figure in the group. Anytime he was absent from the group, we missed his gesturing. Some of us tried to copy him but no one could gesture as much as he did. He had a gesture for almost every word in the dictionary. That was very remarkable.

Sylvia was the typical curious girl. She was the tiniest among us, but obviously not the quietest. She posed a lot of challenging questions which sometimes elicited the need for further research. She could have three sub-questions in one full question by the time she ended. This kept everybody engaged as we all tried to find various responses for her numerous questions. Sylvia also had a way of gesturing approval to encourage members to express themselves fully. She was a strong motivator for the group, always with a smile on her face.

Charles was the calm and quiet type. Looking at his peaceful and serene demeanor, no one credited him with anything. However, this guy was very smart. He would talk less, listen more, and observe critically. Perhaps that explained his fast learning ability. Charles would pick up lessons faster than anybody else in the group. He needed no elaboration in most cases. When it came to remembering past lessons and putting them to work in the group, this guy was there for us. He could reproduce lectures and discussions almost exactly as the tutor did in class. He was a very good imitator, which made him surprisingly funny sometimes. He used to imitate the humorous mannerisms of some of the tutors, and he was so good at it that often we could not differentiate him from the tutor involved. Once in a while he would chip in a funny interjection and send us into gales of laughter. What made him more unique was the fact that, with his calmness, no one expected him to have any sense of humor, and when he showed that side of him, we just could not stop admiring him.

This blend of unique talents and personalities made the "Tseinoo Group" very special and successful. In fact, the way we worked hard, and loved and treated each other with mutual respect and sympathy inspired other students so much so that they wished they had been in our group. We received many requests for admission, but we could consider only one student—Julius—from another class because we did not want to have too large a group as that could impact adversely on our efficiency.

Personally, I discovered a pattern emerge in our sitting positions. I had noticed that anytime the group sat for discussions, Sylvia either took a spot next to me or directly opposite me. Whenever I made a submission or stressed a point during discussion, she would lean slightly forward and look at me approvingly. Even when I found it difficult to put my point across, her look gave me the impression that I was making sense. That encouraged me to actively participate in our discussions. During just about the last official group discussion in the penultimate trimester, Sylvia broke the glass ceiling which caught me unawares. She sat to my right that evening. In the course of the discussion, she put her head on my right shoulder for a brief period and lifted it. A warm sensation ignited in my neck and quickly ran down my spine and out. As usual, I did not show any outward reaction to that but inwardly I froze as I struggled to figure out what that meant.

That was the first time a lady had ever laid her head on my shoulder and I considered it a threat. I started processing it mentally, which took my mind off the discussion. I never knew she was just absolutely overwhelmed by the reasoning in my submission for that evening. She had quite appreciated the way I reasoned out my submission and the methodical presentation of my argument which made my conclusion absolutely unquestionable. Many, many years later I learned that she was so fascinated about my argument and style of presentation that she overlooked the principles underlying our friendship. It was worth letting me know she was proud of me. That was an impulsive way of expressing her admiration. Such impressive display of knowledge and skill on my part subsequently swept her off her feet. Somewhere along the line but unknown to me, I had gotten to be attractive to Sylvia for my deft handling of academic subjects. She was gradually being struck by the Cupid's arrow but there was a problem. Pitch black men like me were not her favorite. Neither was a man from my ethnic group her preference; and someone with such poor interpersonal skills, raw and shy like Aaron, would not be an ideal partner for marriage. Despite all these flaws, Sylvia still could not stop her heart from yearning for me. Later, she confessed that she could not understand why she even fell deeply in love with me in the first place. I was contrary to whatever she desired in her dream man except for my academic brilliance, but she felt strongly that life wouldn't be the same without me. "It felt like something was pushing me from within toward you despite my conscious efforts to resist," she later confessed. Besides, she admired my efforts to attain spiritual growth through my constant daily prayers on the field, leading Bible studies and taking a leadership role (Secretary) in the Scripture Union. She was convinced that my love for God was very strong, an attribute she rated beyond everything in her friends. Moreover, I presided over the Student Representative Council's Project Committee as its Chairman, yet I did all that with a very quiet demeanor and unassuming character.

We all go through fantasy one way or the other, especially about people we admire. Sylvia theorized that children with such a gifted and principled gentleman would be a blessing. *Perhaps we could work on the interpersonal skills,* she dreamed. It turned out that she was spot on: all of our three children are in the Gifted & Talented class of their respective grades. Every end of year, they come home with multiple awards and medals of achievement. Did Sylvia see through time? Women have rare discerning emotions. However, being the principled lady that she was, Sylvia was not willing to damage our friendship by disrespecting the underlying principles. She knew that as principled and disciplined as I was, if she made any relationship gesture to me beyond our prevailing friendship, it would mark the end of our partnership and the collapse of any dream she had of sharing a life with me.

The first time she wanted to give me a gift, she meandered through a third party to avoid offending me or violating our memorandum of understanding. She was genuine but did not know how I was going to interpret her giving me a gift. By sheer wits, she successfully pulled off one of the tricky events that could have, otherwise, gotten me annoyed and out of the friendship. She first talked to Vincent. We were heading toward a Christmas break. One day, on our way to the classroom, Vincent asked me, "What are you offering Sylvia this season by way of a gift?" I told him that I would love very much to offer her a gift, but I did not want her to have the impression that I was interested in a relationship. So, I am not giving any gifts. Then he continued, "What about if she gave you one?" I laughed out loud and told him I would only accept it if it came without seductive motives, but I quickly walked back my words out of respect for Sylvia. I told him not to get me wrong, because I trusted Sylvia's integrity. So far, she had earned my respect for her patience, discipline, and godliness. Then Vincent revealed the main reason for that particular interaction: "She has one for you then," he said. "Are you serious? What is it?" I asked doubtfully. "It is a special sauce aromatically spiced to taste. I bet you will love it," he said. Immediately, one of the Cooperative School rules came into mind: "Do not receive gifts of whatever form especially from unknown sources." I battled with this for a while. *Is Sylvia still a stranger?* I rationalized. It was difficult for me, and I did not want to embarrass her either. I had come to completely trust Sylvia so I took the risk and told Vincent that I would accept her gift. We went straight to Vincent's locker after meals, and I took it. There was an accompanying message that read, "My mother sent me two big containers of this aromatic stew through my elder brother today and I thought of sharing them with you."

In her wisdom, Sylvia had offered another container of the sauce to Vincent with a similar message in order to make me feel comfortable accepting it. Initially, I was both curious and skeptical, but when I saw that she had offered a similar gift to my friend, I dropped my inhibitions completely. Later that evening, I met her in the classroom and thanked her for the gift, but I did not dwell much on it. I quickly shifted attention to our task for that evening. In spite of the success of the Tseinoo Group, Sylvia and I never abandoned our original study partnership. We had separate schedules for our study partnership and that of the group. Most of the time we would meet as a duo for discussion before joining the larger Tseinoo Group for another activity.

THE TSEINOO GROUP
(Left to right) **Standing:** *Vincent, Sylvia, Charles, Sitsofe and I;* **Squatting:** *Julius and Gideon*

Vincent (left) and I on our way to lectures.

CHAPTER 12

ALLEGATIONS AND THE
GOLDEN QUESTION

THE ALLEGATIONS

"Cast not away therefore your confidence, which
hath great recompense of reward."
—Hebrews 10:35 (KJV)

After the next few trimesters, there were some developments that nearly rocked our otherwise very healthy partnership and platonic friendship. Sylvia and I always met in public places, usually the classroom or under tree shade designated for studies. For all the periods we were on campus, we never had a single private meeting where we could be seen in a secluded place. We were very careful and determined not to do anything that would tempt us into any sexual attraction and cause us to betray Christ Jesus and our faith. This made our friendship very public, and the rumors spread fast.

Other students and even some jealous high-profile officials who had seen us always studying together naturally and hastily

109

suspected that we were in a love relationship and that there was some kind of chemistry going on between us. The sincerity that existed between us did not matter to anybody but was misconstrued as an illicit love relationship. This was something that neither of us liked or had intended because such a description cast doubts on what we had professed. Such a notion also ran contrary to what we preached. Sylvia had always maintained that pre-marital sex was wrong and sinful. I had also publicly condemned students who developed immoral relationships on campus. It was, therefore, quite ironic that ours was seen in such same light.

Within this challenge to our study partnership, I faced another individually, customized challenge. I had become the object of hostility from a particular so-called missionary who subsequently doubled as a tutor. Obviously, he did not like my friendship with Sylvia and I did not know why. Until later events on campus pitched him against the Principal of the college on certain suspicions, I could not tell whether the former was jealous or just as ignorant of our friendship as other students were. Anytime he saw me with Sylvia, I observed him frown. He would talk fondly with Sylvia but would not say a single word to me. In our subsequent encounters, I would walk on while he engaged Sylvia in conversation. I hardly interacted with officialdom yet this man's attitude toward me was very hostile even into the exam hall. He also went to the extent of influencing another gullible tutor against me. I got to know this because that lady tutor was close to the missionary who was hostile to me. She once wrote insults on one of my test papers in her subject for expressing an independent opinion she considered wrong. I thought "Personal Response" in literature was a matter of one's individual perspective drawn from a preamble. Surprisingly, it was not so in this woman's view. Where I expressed pity for the person in the poem I was appreciating, she retorted in red ink on my paper, "You should rather pity yourself." "What! Are we in a fight? I thought I submitted an assignment for correction," I exclaimed. I suddenly realized it had something to do with her closeness to the missionary who was hostile to me. Clearly, there was something more to it. I do not know exactly what the missionary told her but common sense revealed that it had to do with my friendship with Sylvia. Prior to this, she barely noticed me in her class. I showed my assignment paper to Vincent and both of us concluded it was very unprofessional for a tutor to get that personal. However, we reasoned that the best way to confront this issue was for me to ignore her and keep my focus. Final exam was approaching. It was not worth spending time on an emotional tutor. We kept our resolution to ourselves and went to work as usual.

Obviously, Sylvia seemed not to be cognizant of this development because of the missionary cloak this man was hiding in. As mature as I was, I did not want her to feel bad for being the cause of my ill-treatment by these officials. I also did not want to influence her opinion about people either, so I kept quiet about it. If she woke up to it and brought it up, then we could discuss it. She never brought it up, so I let sleeping dogs lie. I, however, confided in Vincent who had also noticed it. The ill treatment of these two tutors did not bother me much because they were in the minority. I enjoyed a lot of respect from the majority of the tutors and students who knew my logic and academic strengths.

It did not help either when one of our English Literature set books entitled, *Silas Marner*, virtually set this rumor of our friendship in 3-D. In the book, Silas Marner, who had a daughter called Eppie, had been alienated from society and faith for a considerable period of time. However, his daughter's love relationship with a young man called Aaron finally brought him back to interactions with the community. It looked as if George Elliot, the author, saw through time into our friendship and predicted it in the story.

My name was Aaron, the exact name of the young man who dated Eppie. The description of Eppie in the novel strikingly matched Sylvia's physique, demeanor, and personality. Elliot was almost prophetic. Sylvia, for a period, lost her name on campus. She became widely known as Eppie throughout the college campus. Our juniors, who did not understand her sudden name change, inquired from others and the narrative even made the rumors of our friendship more popular and all the more credible. Many a time, mates would meet me and ask, "Where is Eppie?" That was very tormenting for me, and I wished they could understand the foundation of our friendship. Meanwhile, Sylvia took it cool and rode high in her newfound fame. She was always smiling and gracious as usual, responding to the name Eppie as if it was another derivative of Sylvia. When I asked if it does not bother her, Sylvia argued that fighting it would even make things worse by blowing things out of proportion. She said, "If I start fighting it now, everybody would be asking why. The more the whys, the farther the rumor goes." She was right, of course. We had no choice but to ignore the distraction and focus on our objectives while our fellow students continued referring to us as Aaron and Eppie.

Sometimes, during these challenging periods, I would peel off from Sylvia for no apparent reason other than just to prove that we could stay away from each other any time, any day and neither of us would lose anything. The problem was that such acts put a lot of strain on our friendship because I did so without giving Sylvia any reason or notice. One thing I really admired about her was her wits. I could easily tell what her reaction would be if I told her. She would likely reply that if I was not thinking anything like that, why worry about unfounded allegations? But I felt I needed to prove a point, even if temporarily. However, my actions made her suspect that she might have unconsciously violated some of the principles underlying our friendship.

Whenever she had the opportunity Sylvia asked if she had done anything wrong. I would reply in the negative but would not explain why. I realized this made her very uncomfortable and caused her a lot of pain because such acts tended to derail our otherwise very progressive partnership. Sometimes I could see the stress in her face, but fully aware of the underlying principles of our friendship, Sylvia kept her cool. At times she would just say, "You are pretending!" Still, such an accusation would not draw me out enough to tell her my reason. This on-and-off attitude of mine continued for some time until one day Sylvia approached me out of frustration. Certainly, she knew something was going on with me. Since I was unwilling to tell her the reason for my behavior, she kept on guessing that perhaps she was a bother to me. The next time we met again, she nearly came to tears and sincerely offered to leave me alone if that would make me happy. That evening, I saw another demonstration of genuineness of heart and unselfishness on her part. I got to know that she put my welfare even beyond whatever she stood to gain from our partnership studies. Realizing this completely disarmed me. She was young, but I was fascinated by her mature way of thinking. I decided to abandon trying to prove people wrong and focus on our lessons.

I came to the conclusion that if God did not see us in a bad light, that was enough and all that we needed. However, I was satisfied with the fact that we were largely independent of each other. Sylvia never reacted possessively, which elevated my respect for her as a genuine person. We resumed our consistent studies leaving our observers to continue their conspiracy theory mongering. We concentrated on our objectives and respected our priorities. Mindful of the rumors, we conducted ourselves even more carefully and generally speaking, very well. It is said, "Familiarity breeds contempt" but in our case, it was the opposite. The more familiar we became, the more we respected each other.

Trimesters came, and trimesters went. Sylvia and I grew fonder of each other, yet we absolutely avoided any sinful behavior. Less than two trimesters away from graduation we still held the view that marriage between us was quite impossible even though we cared much about each other. As such, neither of us was willing to put the other's future in jeopardy. In fact, anytime we were not talking academics, we were encouraging each other to stay the godly course. Our primary focus still, was to study together, share ideas, brainstorm, pass our examinations, and graduate. We had no plans beyond that, and we had never talked about life after school so far.

THE GOLDEN QUESTION AND THE MARRIAGE CODE

"Even with a crooked stick, God can hit straight." —Augustine

In the concluding weeks of the penultimate trimester, something symbolic happened. I took notice, but Sylvia was not aware of what had just taken place. There was one thing she did that meant the whole world to me but she had no hindsight. That trimester was mainly for Teaching Practice, a form of internship that gave us a real feeling of what it was like to teach as a professional. We were distributed among the surrounding elementary and middle schools in partnerships of two student-teachers per class. The pairing of students for this purpose was the responsibility of the Education Department. Students were selected at random and paired to maintain the integrity of the process.

Coincidentally, my name had been drawn with Sylvia's when the list came out. A student who did not understand the nature of our friendship reported to the Head of the Education Department that we were in a love relationship and that our pairing presented a potential problem of conflict of interest. The Director of Education called me to find out the veracity of this claim. I took time to explain to him that our partnership was being misconstrued. Ours was not a love relationship as we frequently saw among others on campus. Our relationship was purely based on academic pursuit.

I proved to him that we had never gone out together before, that Sylvia did not know my house, and I had never even put a foot in her hometown, let alone know in which direction her house was. In spite of becoming the best of friends, we had never gone out together before, we had never met anywhere else apart from the areas designated for studies, which were all public places. I dared him to find out any evidence of a single moment we were found in secret or even in lonely places on or outside the campus grounds. I was gradually becoming emotional as I had gotten tired of the nonsense. In the process; I dared him to ask any student who came to make such a complaint to mention anywhere we had been seen or something we had done that suggested we were in a love relationship. In my heart, I truly loved Sylvia as a sister but not to the extent of having a desire of sexual intimacy. "Seeing a lady and a gentleman meet regularly for studies does not connote a sexual relationship, does it?" I asked rhetorically. Notwithstanding this, I asked the Director of Education to assign both of us new partners for the sake of integrity, and to satisfy the doubting Thomases. I could see that he was very relieved at my suggestion. He realized that much as I disapproved of the public perception of our friendship, I was equally concerned about the integrity of his work. He spoke to me with a lot of respect in his voice and thanked me for my sincerity. I came out of his office knowing that I could not please everybody. If I had dwelled on trying to prove myself to everybody, I could have put an unnecessary strain on our otherwise healthy partnership. It rather strengthened my resolve to stick to Sylvia even more. That very evening, I met Sylvia for discussion as usual. I expected her to have heard about the complaint, but since she did not raise it, I did not bring it up either. We concentrated on the evening's tasks and carried on with our work as usual. She had actually heard of the complaint, but in her opinion, she had nothing to prove to anybody. Rumors were not worth investing a minute of her time in, and I admired her strong personal principles.

Later, when the list was revised, the two of us were given different partners. Ironically, we still ended up in the same school for the teaching practice, but we were not teaching partners for the same class. My new partner and I taught in a higher class whereas Sylvia and her new partner taught in a lower class. Each day after closing we would gather together and wait for a bus to take us back to campus. This continued until the last day of the internship when I witnessed something dramatic happen but Sylvia was unaware.

The morning was partly cloudy with clear visibility when we disembarked from our buses. Frantic preparations in the school where we did our internship were going on. The greenery had been shaped and the trees were adorned with decorations. The offices and the classrooms were also decorated. The atmosphere surely reflected that of a ceremony. There were going to be series of performances by the students we taught to mark the closing ceremony. All the interns, including Sylvia and I, were the guests of honor.

At the end of the performances, we brought the month-long exercise to an end. The function closed very early, so we had plenty of time before the bus arrived. We gathered in groups under shady trees chatting about topics of interest and taking pictures. I did not feel like taking one, but for Sylvia's pleasure, I stood with her for a picture that became to me an emblem of what I call the Golden Question. After standing for a while, Sylvia told me her feet were tired and she wanted to sit down. This meant that she had to walk some distance back to the classroom blocks where there were seats. I did not want to leave her all alone, so I offered to keep her company. We walked back to the nearest classroom block and sat down on the veranda at the rear.

After talking to some of the students, we turned to ourselves. For the first time since our acquaintance, we talked about life beyond school. We talked about life at home and some of the challenges we were likely to face after graduation. We were just a trimester away from graduation, so naturally, we were eager to know about our future prospects. Among other things, Sylvia expressed the desire to advance her education to the university level in order to get her bachelor's degree. Memories of my struggle with the "A" Level came back to mind, but I did not tell her about them. Even though she was not going to sit for the same exam, I knew it was not going to be easy for her. I encouraged her to start preparing very early to give herself a head start. She was a product of a new system, the Senior Secondary School Certificate of Examination (SSSCE), which was gradually replacing the old "A" Level system, so I could not really tell her what to expect. I had the intention to do another battle with the "A" Level before it was phased out, and time was running out for me. However, I did not want Sylvia to know my plans, as I was not yet sure if I could pass the "A" Level. When it came to my turn, I remember telling Sylvia I was not afraid of the future because of Christ Jesus. I believed in the promises of the Bible just as I respected the admonishments therein. Therefore, no matter how hard life became, I was sure to weather the storm, mainly because I was convinced God was on my side. "If I lose anything, I am sure to regain it," I said confidently. "Therefore, if anybody struggled with me for even what was legally mine, I would simply let that fellow have it. It would just be a matter of time that I should have a new one or even the very same thing back," I concluded. As soon as I had finished this statement, Sylvia, seemingly oblivious of the import, asked me what I've termed the "Golden Question"—"Would you like to live your life with me?" she asked.

I was absolutely taken aback, but I kept my composure as usual. Perhaps, I thought, she must have discerned something special in me and would not allow that future to slip out of her hands: "Mark the perfect man, and behold the upright: for the end of that man is peace" (Ps. 37:37, KJV). Our focus on godly and laudable future goals in our discussions must have compelled her to check if I could still be there in that future as I was with her in the present. Other than that, we cannot think, even at present, what bearing Sylvia's question had on my submission. She just popped it out from the blue. For a while, I could not utter a word. Though she had no way of knowing it, Sylvia had just blurted out a fulfillment of the most difficult proof of all the signs I had laid out in my covenant.

I held my breath for a while as Sylvia looked at me indifferently. Instead of giving her an immediate answer, I told her, "Let's get out of here! I will talk to you next Tuesday." That conversation was on a Friday. I felt I had to brood very well over the matter in order to arrive at the true interpretation. *Did she ask me? What prompted her to ask me so?* She had respected all the protocols of our friendship for years; why was she now breaking them so boldly and openly? I expected it to come in a statement *but why is it coming in the form of a question?* I could not process my thoughts effectively. I kept praying in my head while we walked away to join the others. The bus arrived, and we boarded en route to campus. That evening was very mixed for me. As usual, I went onto a football (soccer) field to pray after dinner. After prayers, I remained there trying to recollect my covenant and see how Sylvia measured into the details. So far, I had concentrated on the threat and hardly thought of how any woman on campus could fit into the image of my covenant. I thought with solemnity. I played back Sylvia's question in my mind and carefully considered it to figure out what it meant exactly:

"Would <u>you</u> like to live your <u>life</u> with <u>me?</u>"

In asking me this question, Sylvia was clearly indicating the future. She did not ask for a study partner. She already had one in me. She asked for a 'life with me.' What does it mean to live one's life with someone else? I came up with the following key words: *future, life, you,* and *me.* What does this equation mean?

Me + You + Life + Future=?

The most suitable answer I could arrive at was MARRIAGE. How else would a lady propose? That was exactly Sign #2 in my covenant with God. Even though it came camouflaged in the form of a question rather than the open declaration I expected, the substance remained the same. The initiative came from her. Moreover, the indifference in her face when she asked me this question showed that she was unaware of the impact of her own words. She was, indeed, unaware of how sensitive it was to me. Furthermore, her question had little to do with the topic under discussion. All these considerations made me believe that the Golden Question, as well as the friendship that grew out of our study partnership, did not happen at random. There was a divine hand in how the whole thing played out. Clearly, both of us did not want a relationship. We wanted to focus on partnering in studies and studies alone.

Having satisfied myself with the Golden Question, I moved on to consider Sign #1. Sylvia scored great marks for that one as well. I had partnered with her long enough to know much about her commitment to God. I was even surprised about her objectivity since I knew her church to be very dogmatic about certain issues and their biblical interpretations. Anytime her church doctrines came in conflict with reality, she chose practicality. She was one who was looking for the truth at all times. If she found out that something was biblically more practical than her church's position, she would go with her conviction. This stance perfectly agreed with my point of view. Her goal was to please God by knowing His Word and obeying it to the exclusion of anything else. She was someone I could bank on to join me in my quest to honor God all the days of my life.

I moved on to Sign #3. I thought carefully about that while trying to figure out how Sylvia measured up to it. As somebody who had striven to stay sexually pure for decades, I would not like to be cheated on by a partner who had been jumping into every bed. I had no clue how to judge whether someone was a virgin or not. I also did not want to ask around because I could be lied to. Moreover, people might figure out what I was up to. Therefore, I resorted to reconsidering our various interactions as far back as I could remember and gleaned from it statements that alluded to chastity or otherwise. I spent a great deal of time trying to remember the Immemorable, yet I struggled to get any sentence that implicated her. Sylvia had never made any statement that showed she had ever had a relationship in the past with any gentleman or was ever in one at any time. I remembered she once told me during one of our discussions that this was the closest she had ever come to any man apart from her father. That statement was significant in my quest to establish the truth about her. She hardly ever talked about men except to tell me of their immoral requests and their advances, which she detested. By observing my discreet behavior and personal principles in the course of our friendship, Sylvia had reposed complete trust in me. She was emboldened to disclose personal matters of trust to me because she knew I would never take advantage of her. I reckoned her innocence, and I was very careful not to betray that trust. I took those disclosures, especially her innocent behaviors, as signs of virginity and *presto!* The awareness dawned on me suddenly. *Why did I not notice all that far back in our interactions?* I asked myself. I burst into prayer once again, thanking God for the revelation and keeping His promise. I made an offer to God that, should we succeed in marriage, I would take this testimony as far as I can to encourage believers to absolutely keep trusting Him. This is the reason why you are reading this book or having it read to you. It has taken us more than a decade to compile our experiences to encourage you in this direction. You may think I was going to declare to Sylvia my discovery about her right away but no. It would still be eight more years before she would know.

I came back from the soccer field that evening still in a state of shock. Sometimes, we pray to God for something but when it arrives, we cannot even believe it is happening. I was simply not ready for it. *How come something we had thought an impossibility all this while was suddenly possible after all?* I could not bring myself to reason with the sudden turn of events. I remained calmer than my original calmness. Even so, I felt some gladness in my inner being. I kept thinking things through and wondering about them. That evening I was late to the classroom for our usual appointment as the prayer and analysis had taken more of my time than usual. When I saw Sylvia, my mood was a mixture of solemnity and gladness. My reactions in our interactions were smooth and steady but I was slower than my usual self. Sylvia felt it immediately and asked if I was tired from the day's activities. I answered in the negative. She did not know that my perspective about her had changed. She looked even more graceful and pleasant to behold than ever, but I made no overt expression of that. I had still not completely recovered from my shock, but I was full of gratitude for the turn of events. I knew I was going to marry; better still, I knew who my future wife was going to be. Nothing could be more exact. God had answered my prayer in exactly the way I proposed it in the covenant. It was fascinating to realize I had been talking to my future wife all this while and did not know it. The end my fear of seduction was in sight.

By the next Monday, I had already penned down what I was going to touch on during our meeting the next day. It was tough for me, but I knew I had to say something to Sylvia. I had to react to her 'Golden Question" which I deemed to be a proposal, and that was the scary part for me. In all my interactions, the word *love* had never proceeded from my mouth, either to her or to any other lady. I was very cautious about my diction for fear of misinterpretation. If there is one English word that had been so misconstrued, it was *love* hence I was very careful about its use. It hardly ever came out of my mouth in my interactions. But then I realized I may have to use it or else what would be the basis of my response? I struggled to get myself to violate my own principle in that sense. Even so, I managed to circumvent it by resorting to the words 'like' and 'desire' instead.

At long last, the day came. I began to feel jittery about the whole thing, yet a kind of happiness also permeated through me at the same time. I was not too eager, but my happiness was undented. After lunch, I managed to brush off all my inhibitions and went to the classroom where we were supposed to meet. I sat down and prayed. Moments after, Sylvia came in and we sat opposite each other. We prayed briefly, and I set the ball rolling. I do not remember all I said. However, I remember drawing Sylvia's attention to the fact that we were there because we had agreed the previous Friday to meet for an interaction other than an academic one.

This was the first time something of this kind was happening. We had been friends for a long time, and we knew much about each other. Yet, I still wanted to know if she was really interested in living with a queer guy like me. She replied by advising me not to describe myself like that because she did not see me that way. She described me as a fine gentleman whose intelligence she had come to like. There was not a single meeting in which she was not fascinated by my way of thinking, my logical presentation of facts, and especially my uncompromising character, which made me a very hard nut to crack. She declared that I made most of the things she did not understand in class look very easy during our discussions. Above all, she dearly admired my love for God and my active participation in the Scripture Union. To her, I did not appear in any way like I was describing myself. She continued that she could not tell what was happening to her but that some time back she felt like she could not live without me and could not concentrate on our work together. But, over the period she learned to deal with it even though she still could not tell how she would feel without me.

"It will be hard, but at the same time I admire your principles and I want to respect you as such," she concluded.

It was then that I knew the grounds were already prepared long before I got the first glimpse of our changed relationship. Knowing what I knew then, I felt more confident and told her I would like to have her as my wife in the future but that I could not imagine her as a sexual partner yet. Such a notion made me feel very, very bad and consciously guilty. It would take many more years for me to make that transition before our marriage. Sylvia leaned forward, rubbed the back of my left hand, which was on the desk, and in a very low voice, she interrupted, "I think I love you, dear." I quickly cut in with the following correction, "No, you don't just think, you really do love me. Maybe, you are afraid you may offend me. You just said life without me may be hard for you. That is not a thought. It is real, your real desire." I concluded. She looked at me with a smile and said, "You just exhibited one of the reasons why I need you around me. You take issues and put them in the right perspective and you are not afraid to do so regardless of who is in front of you. That is how I feel but I could not describe it as ideally as you have." I smiled back at her in agreement. I began to reveal to her more about myself. I told her about my fears but not the reasons behind them.

Marriage with Sylvia was possible, but it would take a considerable number of years to bring this to pass. I warned her to be ready for surprises because she would not be liked by everybody in my family. I made her aware that my mother, in particular, detested girls from her region, and if it were left to Auntie Aggie alone, her children would never marry anyone from Sylvia's neck of the woods. In the same way, I warned Sylvia to beware of the fact that even if it was not evident at that time, she would likely encounter opposition from her own family if she mentioned marriage with an Ashanti man.

What was more, I was not at all ready for marriage financially, so it would take a lot of time for me to prepare for that. Therefore, I wanted her to bear in mind that our possible union was still miles away from reality. While marching toward that goal, I advised Sylvia to pursue her bachelor's degree as she had indicated. I was also going to do the same as soon as I got out of school. Hopefully, by the time we got our bachelor's degrees, my marriage preparation would be complete; then we could tie the knot, God willing. However, I warned her that things could change. We did not know the future, so she should keep her gears still in the neutral position and let us pray. God is truthful, and His will would bring us together if He approved of it. I never gave Sylvia any hint of my own covenant and how she fulfilled it. I was determined to hide it from her and from everyone else until our marriage had become a reality. That would be my first wedding gift. I could see a big smile of gratitude in her face. Her spirit was lifted. She gazed at me with her lovely eyes behind her glasses. Sylvia would have kissed me if she could, but she knew that I would not allow that. She pulled my nose as was her custom even with other members of the Tseinoo Group. She would do that to anybody she loved. At one point in time, we had to hold our noses as soon as we finished group discussions. It was a given that Sylvia was going to pull your nose if you left it unguarded—Sitsofe was a regular victim of hers in this respect. We prayed again and before we parted, I told Sylvia to keep all that had transpired between us very secret; not even her parents should hear about it. She nodded in agreement, saying she would be very careful with that. What I liked about Sylvia was her discretion. I knew I could trust her to do exactly that, and she did. As you will later read, we kept this between the two of us for more than five years before her parents even became aware of it. We left the classroom beaming cheerfully with the hope that graduation may not be the end of our friendship and our partnership. We knew our life together was a long way off, but as long as we were on course, we were happy with it. We still thought it inexpedient to get into a relationship then. We maintained the usual casualness of our friendship, avoiding any temptation to kick it up to a closer relationship.

Each of us respected our individual selves, hence decency came naturally into our interactions. Neither of us was willing to betray the trust of the other. I was aware that we were still not done yet. In between, anything could happen to jeopardize my covenant. I saw that coming period as the most critical. Now that we had openly declared our interest in each other, the temptation to sin by way of a sexual relationship was even greater; therefore, we needed to exercise far more greater restraint. Thank God, I still saw Sylvia more as a sister and felt nothing about her as a sexual partner. Besides, she was very innocent, even vulnerable. That being the case, I felt even more duty bound to protect that innocence than ever before. I remembered that Sylvia had originally come to me partly to seek refuge from some gentlemen who had preyed on her. I felt, therefore, more obliged to keep that trust than ever.

Moreover, I had not spoken to Sylvia's father yet, so I had no right to go after her. I was quite aware that spiritually, this mattered a lot. The father is the umbrella over his children, and until I had introduced myself to him and sought his blessing, I could never remove that spiritual covering over her. It would have grievous spiritual consequences if I did, and I was not ready for such. Consequently, we could not go any further with our friendship than where it was at that time. It took four years for God to reveal to me the fact that I would marry and to whom. Incredibly, it would take twice as many years to see the realization of this dream. I had to exercise a lot of patience, and it was very worth it. That trimester ended, and our vacation exchanges became more frequent than previously. We kept encouraging each other to stay the course and shared biblical exhortations as usual until we returned for the last and final trimester in college.

*Sylvia and I at the end of our internship, a picture
that has become the symbol of the "Golden Question."*

CHAPTER 13

THE FINAL TRIMESTER

"But even more blessed are all who hear the word of God and put it into practice."
—Luke 11:28 (NLT)

The final trimester began in earnest and Sylvia and I could not wait to see each other. I arrived on campus in the late evening after sunset. Sylvia had arrived earlier in the day and waited anxiously. Any time she heard a group of students had arrived from Kumasi, she would rush over to see if I was among them. Mobile telecommunication was not common in those days. Even if it were, we were not rich enough to own a mobile phone then, so we could only communicate face-to-face or through snail mail. At last, I arrived among the last batch of students from Kumasi. Sylvia was quick to come to the scene and waved at me to signal her presence. I was equally happy to see her. I could not wait to put my luggage in my locker and come out to meet her.

Our first encounter was full of excitement. We shared our experiences during the vacation. Even though we had shared most of them in our mail exchanges, we still loved to hear them again. We

127

had already discussed through the mail our resolution to make that final trimester count very much. Soon, we would be writing our final examination so that evening was the only chance we had to chat heartily. The next day we would resume full academic workload and studies. At nightfall, we had to part to our dormitories in order to clean up and prepare for our first lessons the next day. It was sad to leave but we had to go as we hoped to see each other the next day.

The trimester was loaded both on the academic calendar and our personal study calendar. Our group study calendar also made it even tighter to get a breather. Sylvia and I worked through it knowing that both of us were aiming higher.

The final examinations came in June 1998. We took them one subject at a time. By the grace of God, none of us reported anything particularly bothersome. In the last days, I made Sylvia stick more with Vincent than myself. I did that for a reason. Sticking out with her too much would send the wrong signal about our relationship beyond what we were already known for, and, if I was not sticking out with Sylvia, I would not like her to feel abandoned either. I had a camera with me in the last trimester, but I took more pictures of Sylvia with Vincent than myself with her. For the sake of decency, I always posed for a picture with her with either another lady or another gentleman in attendance. On only a few occasions would we take pictures alone as a duo.

In June 1998, the last day finally arrived and we had to depart. It was an emotional moment but we could not avoid it. On the eve of our departure, Sylvia and I arranged to meet for the last time on campus. It was in the evening after supper. We still chose to sit in public on a parapet by the edge of the main street that came into the campus. We had a long conversation as Sylvia would leave the next dawn. At 8:00 P.M. that night, I had to attend my last Scripture Union meeting. We wished each other the best and set out on our way.

At the point where we were supposed to part ways, we stopped and still kept talking. Sylvia mentioned how greatly she would miss me, but I encouraged her to have faith in God and trust that we would be together in the future. We were parting ways for a while, and she could always reach out to me by mail. She gave a melancholic smile, shook my hands, and pulled my nose. Then, she turned toward the girls' dormitory. I stood still and watched her as she strode under the street lights. When she turned once and saw me looking at her, she giggled and continued onward. At the gate, she turned once again toward my direction and waved for the last time before entering the dormitory. I then turned to go to the Scripture Union meeting. I was about eight minutes late.

After the meeting, I said goodbye to the brothers and sisters in Christ that I was leaving behind and gave out my address and contact information. I returned to my cubicle very tired and exhausted. Still, I had one more assignment—to draft a farewell message for Sylvia and Sitsofe, the only two faithful ladies in the Tseinoo Group. I picked a chair and sat at a desk as I carefully drafted very touching messages for these ladies. I read, reviewed, and redrafted until I had perfected my messages. I had sat very deep into the night. Sylvia's bus would be leaving at 4:00 A.M. If I wanted to catch her before she left, I had to wake up earlier. I threw myself on my bunk bed and slowly drifted into dreamland.

The next day, each of the members of the Tseinoo Group departed at various times. Sylvia was the first person to leave. At dawn, I dropped her the note I had drafted the previous night while she was on the bus. In the note I had penned some emotional farewell messages. I had also indicated that it was still possible that situations may change rendering us unable to see each other again. She should, therefore, hold her heart in the neutral gear while still trusting God to guide our dreams into reality. I just did not know when, but even if we did not meet again, I was still grateful to God I had met her. I appreciated her friendship, sincerity, and godliness.

I admitted that Sylvia had taught me a lot about ladies that I previously did not know. She also helped me overcome my shyness to a large extent. I drew her attention to the fact that if I was then talking freely with other ladies on campus, it was because I'd gained confidence by interacting with her. I took her criticisms in good faith, and my interpersonal skills became better than when I first stepped on campus, even though I still had a long way to go. I also dropped a similar parting message for Sitsofe. For the men, I went to each of them, had a hearty chat, a hug, and farewell exchanges before they each departed. In the course of the day, all the members of the Tseinoo Group departed, leaving me alone on campus. I did not leave until the next day as I was waiting for Abraham, my brother, to pick me up on his way to the capital.

At home, it was going to take more than three months before I could even know where I was posted to teach. Meanwhile, exactly two weeks after arrival from campus, I received a letter from Sylvia. She indicated how emotional she became after reading my note. She could not hold back her tears and kept thinking about the future. That evening, I wrote a very lengthy reply encouraging her to remain faithful and serve God to the best of her ability. By His will, we should come together again, even as a couple. In the meantime, we should pay attention to our desire to climb further on the academic ladder.

PART IV

CHAPTER 14

CONQUERING MY NEMESIS AT LAST AND BEYOND

It is not the circumstances in which we find ourselves that matters,
but the spirit with which we meet them that defines our comfort.
—Araba Season

In the very year that I first arrived on Mount Mary college campus, it was announced that the West African Examination Council (WAEC)'s General Certificate of Examination System would be phased out within the ensuing four years. That meant the last "A" Level examination would take place in 1999; luckily, that would be a year after my graduation from college. I would, therefore, have a full year of studies if I wanted to write the 'A' Level exam again before it became extinct. I nurtured the desire to give it a shot for the last time. If I failed to excel and did not beat the competition to make it to the university, that would be the end of the road for me. I would have to look elsewhere for inspiration in other pursuits. I strongly felt that I needed to give it a shot, but I was not sure if I would. I did not have the enthusiasm, the financial wherewithal, or the requisite study materials at that point. I was a willing but helpless soul, so I considered the various options open for me. I realized that the new system of education, the Senior Secondary School Certificate of Examination (SSSCE) to which Sylvia belonged, offered a better chance at the university than the "A" Level offered me. Chances were that Sylvia could end up at the university while I still languished in the wilderness of academic life. It would not feel good when your future wife had a bachelor's degree and you had nothing but an inferior academic credential to show, not when you are the man.

For a period of time, I felt depressed as I thought my way out into the academic future was narrow and limited. My exploits at the training college had renewed my appetite for academic pursuits but I felt a dead end approaching. The surest way to revive my higher academic future was the "A" Level, which was also my nightmare. The cave I was afraid to enter happened to be the only one that held the treasure I sought; that was exactly how it felt at that time. This drove me into intense prayer and searching, as I cried profusely to God to make an opening for me.

A few weeks after that prayer, I was laboring in Azay's fabric material store when my old high school mate, Fokuo, entered. He was the very person who got "arrested" by the Holy Spirit as I've related in chapter five. For more than five years, our paths had never crossed. Fokuo intimated that he was in his final year at the university. I asked him how he did it, because I knew he struggled even more than I with the "A" Level. My desire to retry the "A" Level for the fifth and final time was given a huge boost after our encounter. While I managed to get a pass, which could not beat the high competition for the universities, Fokuo totally failed. He wasn't even in the competition at all. So, if he could turn things around so as to gain admission to the university, then, logically, I stood even a better chance. I made the determination to seek more information and register to retest for the "A" Level for the last time. Within a week, I had followed Fokuo's lead in talking to a private tutor who doubled as a mentor. I also remembered my friend, Bismarck, who also expressed interest in writing the "A" Level while we were in college. I reached out to him about my decision and he came on board. Later he became the Sylvia of my "A" Level studies. He effectively partnered with me, and we challenged ourselves extremely. Every single day of the year we pounced on books like hungry wolves in the midst of a flock.

In the first quarter of 1999, we managed to register to write the last version of the "A" Level in November/December of that year. After a year of relentless studies while teaching at the same time, we sat for the examination and what a success it was!

I made a string of *A* grades in all the subjects I wrote. My study partner, Bismarck, also made all *A*'s with the exception of one in which he made a *B*. When I first saw my exam results with a lineup of *A*'s, I heaved a sigh of vindication, but I did not celebrate. I felt it was long overdue. Some of my former colleagues at the Sixth Form had completed their master's and doctorate degrees already. I was then going to start my bachelor's. It was good but was no fun for me. I thought I was lagging too far behind despite my resurgence. This is how the devil steals our gratitude from us. Sometimes we live in the shadows for so long a time that when we finally come out, we do not appreciate the fact that God has done us good.

One dawn, I wondered why I was unable to rejoice despite achieving what I had been chasing all these years. I got up to pray and immediately something dawned on me, which further deepened my belief in our destiny. I asked myself the reason why it had taken me so long to overcome the "A" Level examination. *What was the reason for the marking of time? Was I dumb?* The answer was negative, because I had overcome the "A" Level with the same mental ability with which I went to Mount Mary College and it showed. '*So, what might have been the real reason?*' I kept pondering.

Then, one question ignited my insight. *Why did I overcome the "A" Level only after I had been to Mount Mary College? Was it the courses I pursued in that college that helped me to succeed in the "A" Level?* I tried hard to discern any link between the two.

Unfortunately, I could not effectively link them. The "A" Level course, and for that matter its syllabuses, were highly designed to prepare students for the pursuit of a bachelor's degree at the university level. Consequently, students of this system had no clearer choice after completion than to continue to the university for their bachelor's. Courses in the Teacher Training Colleges, on the other hand, were specifically designed to prepare students mainly for the teaching profession. Once their course of study was completed, students were posted to teach in elementary and junior high schools. The courses in these institutions were, therefore, mainly pedagogical and specialized. Obviously, the Training College concept and the "A" Level system had very little in common. I concluded that there could be something more to my success than just the Training College experience.

Then, something struck me like lightning. My experience with Sylvia rushed into my mind. *Is there any way we could have still met if I had not gone to the Training College? Hardly!* Sylvia was at the coast and I was in the forest zone, hundreds of miles apart. *Is there any way we could have met if I had not gone at the time I went? Probably never!* After college, we still went back to our respective regions and remained put. *Would a relationship have developed even if I could have met her outside the college campus?* This was a definite no. I was very much wary of seduction hence developing a close relationship with the opposite sex was highly impossible. *Was my success at the "A" Level conditioned upon my acquaintance with Sylvia?* That was highly probable. So, I considered it in detail.

Clearly, I was miles ahead of Sylvia on the academic echelon. And we were schooled in different regions of Ghana, separated by hundreds of miles. I had never traveled to the region where she was born, bred, and schooled. I had no connection whatsoever in that region. There was no way we could have met if everything had gone smoothly for me. Chances are that we would never have met at all. The academic wilderness of my life began to resonate with me. If my struggles with the "A" Level had not happened, how was I going to have a date with my destiny? The terms of my covenant would never have been fulfilled, and I might have remained a bachelor even unto this day. If God had not blocked my entry into the university at that time, I would never have considered Mount Mary College. If I had not gone to Mount Mary College, I would not have met Sylvia. If I had not met Sylvia, there would not be any fulfillment of God's promise in my life. And, if there was no covenant fulfillment, my faith in God would not have been this strong. Everything seemed like a plot that had not been revealed to me prior; and I was blindly guided to play my role in the entire episode. I realized that I was made to mark time for her to catch up with me.

> "This is what the Lord says—your Redeemer, the
> Holy One of Israel:
> "I am the Lord your God, who teaches you what is
> good for you
> and leads you along the paths you should follow." —
> Isa. 48:17. (NLT)

Throughout my childhood, through the academic wilderness, through my vows, through my life on the college campus and the challenges I faced, God was surely teaching me what was good for me and He had divinely led me along the paths I needed to follow. At the same time, He was preparing my future partner for me. He was fine-tuning her life's principles and spiritual development to synchronize with those of mine, to ultimately culminate in our future match up and compatibility.

After such enlightenment, I got up and readied myself for the business of the day. Gladness began to fill my heart again. I was grateful and happy I had annihilated my long-time enemy. The way to the university was not just opened, the institutions were going to fight for me. I had to be glad and look forward to seeing what would become of Sylvia and me. I felt confident and boastful, but I resisted the urge. I remained calm and humble instead. I would not even tell Sylvia about it. It was a battle well fought over a period of about nine years.

THE BIG, PLEASANT SURPRISE

> *"Many people will walk in and out of your life, but*
> *only true friends will leave footprints in your heart."*
> —Eleanor Roosevelt

One day, in early spring of the year 2000, more than a year after our graduation from college, our home phone rang in the morning. I was the only one in the house and was about to leave for Azay's shop. I picked up the phone. As soon as I said, "Hello," a feminine voice on the other end screamed, "I am here, in your city! Where are you?" I hesitated, trying to figure out who this voice (which seemed to have recognized mine) belonged to. The voice came again almost simultaneously, "It's me. Sylvia. I am in Kumasi." My heart just flipped. It was absolutely unexpected. I was so surprised that I did not know what to say. She did not tell me she would be coming to Kumasi. She had arrived the previous day to visit her father. I quickly asked her to head toward the main artery by which access is gained into the suburb where her father lived. I set aside my assignment for that morning and zoomed out of the house. I got into Azay's Mercedes sedan and took off. As I approached the area, I kept scanning. Close to the end of the main route, somebody stood out. I fixed my gaze on that figure throughout.

As I drew close, it became clearer and clearer. It was Sylvia, as cute and pleasant as usual. I stopped and asked her to sit down. With the rumored experience we had on campus, we decided not to expose ourselves as lovebirds even if we had nothing to hide. To avoid prowling eyes, we turned toward an elementary school in the outskirts and parked near a field. We left the car and walked a bit further onto the field. Still guided by decency, we stood in the open field and chatted. We shook hands but did not embrace. Sylvia was as elated to see me as I was glad to hear her voice again. She needed to improve her grades on a few subject areas of the SSSCE. She had, therefore, come to seek her father's assistance in this regard. Improving her grades would launch her into a bachelor's degree hunt in one of the universities.

That was the first time Sylvia and I had met at a place that was not on campus. I was glad she was pushing hard to further her education. It would give us more time to plan and to see God's provision for our lives. I reiterated the need to still keep our friendship under wraps since we were still miles away from marriage. I also made her understand that, should she change her mind in future, she was free to go, hence there was no need to get too intimate. After an hour, I drove her back to where I picked her up for her to walk home. I wished I could drop her right at her doorstep but neither of us wanted to be seen in the company of the opposite sex especially by close relatives. As I drove off, I looked back at Sylvia intermittently through the rearview mirror. Any time I did, I realized she, too, could not keep her eyes off the vehicle. I visited her one more time before she left Kumasi. The second time round, she showed me the house in which her father resided. It was about three blocks away, but we did not venture near for the same reasons as before.

That was the last time I would see Sylvia before she left for Winneba again. We talked about how important it was to shield this friendship from prowling eyes to avoid discouragement or wrong motivation. She was still not aware of my vows, but she spoke through her emotions and convictions. She hoped we would end up marrying, but I had no doubt we would. However, how could we convince people, even our parents, from thinking we were not fornicating? Almost every courtship I had known had involved a sexual relationship at one time or another. We really could find no way we could avoid people's assumptions. Nevertheless, we agreed that we had the responsibility to keep the relationship strictly godly as an example of believers. "Don't let anyone think less of you because you are young. Be an example to all believers in what you say, in the way you live, in your love, your faith, and your purity" (1 Tim. 4:12 NLT)

Both of us agreed that it would be a fitting tribute to God to be able to tell others we stayed the godly course until marriage. It was something we cherished and looked forward to. It would enable us to testify to the youth that contrary to the prevailing notion, with God it was still possible to stay sexually pure. To keep the sanctity of our friendship, we decided to keep it very secret while we went about our lives as marriage was still a long way off. We had to get our bachelor's degrees first, and we were determined to keep that promise to each other until we realized them in our lives.

In the fall of the year 2000, I entered the campus of the University of Ghana. I enrolled in the School of Business to pursue a bachelor's degree in Business Administration. I had specialized in literature and pedagogical skills at the Training College. However, considering the hard rocks that I had hit but had bounced back stronger than before, I felt there was nothing that I could not overcome. I was determined to do business in the future; and I chose to study business courses at the university and major in Financial Accounting. I went with Bismarck, then my bosom friend, who had also obtained excellent grades. It was only after I had arrived on campus that I informed Sylvia of my success. That inspired her to get to the next level. I continued corresponding with her as usual.

Chapter 15

Turbulence Brewed In A Good Year

Will Your Anchor Hold in the Storms of Life? —Priscilla Jane
Owens (1829-1907)

In general, the academic year 2001–2002 was a good one. I
had entered my second year in the university. Sylvia wrote to
me telling me she had been admitted to the University College
of Winneba where her father previously taught. I was very glad
we were both living up to our dreams. It meant we could both
have our bachelor's degrees before tying the knot. Another piece
of good news was that the other members of the Tseinoo Group
had arrived on the campus of the University of Ghana, to pursue
language courses for their bachelor's degrees. I was very happy
to see Vincent, Charles, Sitsofe, and Gideon join me on campus. I
had gained admission to the university a year earlier. Moreover, the
"A" Level covered all first year courses and beyond so I began my
university courses at the second year level. This created a two-year
gap between them on one hand and myself on the other. However,

141

it did not make any difference as we still related to each other in the spirit of the Tseinoo Group.

In that same year, I paid a visit to Sylvia on the campus of the University College of Winneba. That was my first ever journey to Sylvia's hometown. I went to the campus and waited for her at the reception area. She was in a group discussion, but as soon as she heard I had arrived, she left the discussion and came to me. I was astonished when she appeared. She was in many ways different from the Sylvia I once knew. More than two years had passed since I last saw her in Kumasi. Over the time period, Sylvia had put on more flesh and had a wider hip. She had grown into an extremely adorable young lady. All her girly characteristics had disappeared. She was even more adorable to behold, but I did not tell her to her face. I, however, admired her very much. I must confess that I was charmed by her cute lips, smooth arms, and her beautiful bust. Her overall soft-looking cheeks and the whites of her beautiful eyes behind her glasses invaded my thoughts. She took me to the beach where we sat under a round hut and had a hearty chat over a malt drink.

Since that was the first time I was in her hometown, she took the opportunity to give me a brief visual tour and description of the town. We hovered over a wide range of topics, including academia, while we observed the fishermen returning from their previous night's expeditions. Suddenly, Sylvia asked me if I wanted to see her house and greet her mother. I was not ready to show my face in her house yet. Upon her persuasion, however, I agreed to go for her sake. We went back to town and to her parents' house. Mr. Dadzie was in Kumasi still but Mrs. Dadzie was in the house to welcome us. Sylvia introduced me as her best friend. Shyness got the better of me, so I could not talk much. Sylvia and I sat under a tree planted in the middle of the compound. Her mother served us meals and seemed rather happy. It looked as if she knew something about me. I admired Mrs Dadzie's enthusiasm and spirit of service. She was a pleasant woman who did everything she could to make me feel at ease. I realized she saw my shyness, and she tried to get me to talk to her. Beyond that, I believed Mrs Dadzie was also curious about what made Sylvia bring me home. It was something unusual of her daughter. Her reaction made me sense that, as an adult, she figured out what Sylvia and I were up to. Sylvia was exceptionally high spirited while I remained mainly shy. Now that I've matured, I know we just gave ourselves away that afternoon.

From then on, I realized we had gone beyond friendship. We had finally entered into a relationship—at least, Mrs. Dadzie was then aware of it. Sylvia gave me a very beautiful picture of herself as a souvenir. She absolutely looked gorgeous and I felt very proud that such a beautiful girl loved me. I was very happy about the visit. That evening, I wrote a poem to commemorate this day and event.

Upon returning to campus, a cloud of melancholy surrounded my thinking. Our friendship was becoming a relationship. It will surely lead to marriage, yet, in spite of Sylvia's beauty and the development of adorable feminine features, I still could not fathom how I could have any sexual relationship with her. I really loved her but as a blood sister and had enjoyed doing everything for her in that capacity. I had once told Vincent that I wished Sylvia were my mother's daughter. Thinking of her as a future wife gave me strange and uncomfortable feelings even though I loved the idea. I could not bring myself to think that I could ever sleep with her. It felt too unfair an idea to me, even somehow wicked on my part. I was happy to be friends with Sylvia but not so much as a sexual partner. I did not visit Sylvia again before the year ended.

Then came the year 2003, my final year at the University. I visited Sylvia only once during the spring that year. Otherwise, we largely stayed in touch by phone. Our communication became more frequent as we both had acquired cell phones by then. However, we remained significantly distant from each other. I was on the verge of obtaining my bachelor's degree in Business Administration. I visited Sylvia one more time and we discussed whether or not we should come out of the shadows, and if yes, when? It was inconclusive as we could not guarantee the sanctity of the relationship if it became public. We feared that if our relationship became public too early, some forces—whether in our families, our churches, or among our friends—might push us to move faster than we should or hinder our efforts and delay our march toward matrimonial union. Even worse was the fact that we might be discouraged from pursuing the relationship altogether, especially on Sylvia's side. I was privy to God's fulfillment of my covenant, but she was not. I would not do anything to persuade her either, as I wanted divine providence to prove Himself. If God was indeed guiding us through this affair, He would not need my help. Naturally, we should be drawn to each other. Sylvia was also in school still, so I pushed for the idea that our relationship should begin after she obtained her bachelor's. She did not like it much, but Sylvia understood my sense of fairness in the suggestion. Still, we agreed to keep our relationship on a low profile.

A few weeks after my graduation, I was still on campus when Sylvia called and informed me that she had arrived in Kumasi at her father's abode. At this point, she expressed the desire to acquaint herself with key personalities in my family, especially my mother. I did not like the idea entirely but it was a very good idea, so I came on board with her. I agreed to come down and visit her in her father's abode first. Then, I would officially invite her to come over to my house later. We would then have the opportunity to visit my mother to satisfy Sylvia's desire to meet my family members. About a week later, I returned home to Kumasi. The next day, I visited Sylvia in her father's abode, We reviewed our plan, but I was skeptical about it. In order not to hurt Sylvia's feelings, I kept my skepticism to myself as we agreed to carry our plan out. Sylvia was her parents' only daughter and very much attached to her father. Suddenly, here is a strange boy from a notorious city like Kumasi coming to invite Mr. Dadzie's only beloved daughter to a home where only God knows what happens there. Mr. Dadzie had no knowledge of me, my family, or where I lived. I tried to put myself in his shoes to figure out what I would have done if I were in his shoes. In fairness to him, I concluded that I would never leave my beloved virgin daughter in the hands of an energetic young man I never knew even if he came from heaven. It was even more predictable when dealing with a man as principled as Mr. Dadzie.

Four days later, I went to see her. Fortunately, Sylvia's younger brother had also come down to spend some days with their father. I quickly thought to include him in the invitation. I theorized that if I invited Sylvia in the company of her brother, Mr. Dadzie would be less skeptical about me. Hopefully, this would improve our chances of success. I was wrong. Mr. Dadzie would not allow his daughter to leave home with a barely known young man in a city she was not adequately familiar with, not even in the company of the police. My fears came true, so I asked permission to leave. I drove to my mother's house to see how she was faring. From there, I went back home. I had been sorely disappointed but not unexpectedly. I was worried about how Sylvia was going to take it. She was the one who was even more disappointed and embarrassed. For days, I would neither call nor pick up her phone calls. I did not want her father to sense that we were still in touch, because I interpreted his action to mean he was not in favor of the relationship. To scare the bird is not the best way to catch it, so I tried to distant myself to protect Sylvia from his wrath in case he felt angered.

Unfortunately, Sylvia interpreted my distance to mean I was no longer interested in her. Down within my heart I was still very convinced Mr. Dadzie would come on board somewhere along the line. There is no way any man could preempt God's purpose for His son. I could not tell how it would come to be, but I was sure it was going to happen. We just needed a little more time for God to change Mr. Dadzie's mind. Nevertheless, that incident sucked oxygen out of our relationship. We were left with our faith, principles, and discipline to carry us through the next few weeks.

Thankfully, I was quite mature at this stage and able to hold my own. I composed a lengthy letter to Sylvia spelling out my disgust, apprehension, hopes, and the difficult terrain ahead. In the end, I encouraged her to keep the faith still. What really made her suspect that I was going to quit the relationship was my analogy that if her father was that protective of her, I was afraid he was still going to interfere in our marriage even years after he let her out. But that was exactly what I was not ready for; I was not even going to allow my own bossy mother into my marriage were she alive. If we could not resolve our differences among the two of us, then it would not be resolved. That was my position. As an introvert, the last thing I wanted was my marriage affairs getting into the knowledge of a third person. I had made a commitment to God that even if the choice of a lady turned out to be a mistake, I was ready to live with my mistake till death and not tell anybody I made a mistake. I was, therefore, not ready for any compromises or intrusions. I firmly concluded in my submission that in spite of all that, if Sylvia was willing to go along with me, I was more than ready to stick with her no matter the challenge. My promise to her was secure. I was not going to back down. If there should be any backing off, it would never come from my end. With that, I ended my letter.

On her side, Sylvia became so upset that she refused to talk to anybody, even her beloved father. She cut her visit short and returned to Winneba. She wept bitterly after she returned to her mother. Worse was the fact that I was not taking her calls let alone calling her myself. Her mother empathized with her and consoled her. She asked her daughter to be patient, promising that if I were genuine in my love for her, I would return one day. Shortly after that reassurance, my lengthy letter arrived. Sylvia wept when she read it. However, it spurred her on with the determination to confront her father and make him aware that if such incidents that may ruin her life continued, she would not take kindly to that. If she lost me because of him, he would not be blameless if her life got shattered. She was that emphatic. I was far away in Kumasi but I had become the subject of a rift between a beloved father and his young daughter. This is something I never knew.

To overcome a stumbling block, one must look beyond it. So, one evening after weeks of silence, I finally decided to call Sylvia. I was anxious to know what was going on with her. I knew she would be struggling with the issue, but I could not call her just to offer solace either. I was afraid if I continued to communicate with her, I may compound the situation for her.

Sylvia wept on the other end, thinking I may finally quit on her. I directed her to read the concluding part of my letter, which read, "As long as you are willing to go along with me, I will stick to you no matter what." So, the onus was on her. What we needed was time, I convinced her. That seemed to have recovered her hopes significantly. She told me she understood my point very well and that she was working it out with her parents. She continued that my fears for her were unfounded as her parents were not as possessive as I had thought. It was just that she did not handle her part very well before I came, and her father did not do a good job either. He could have handled it better knowing she was no longer the girl child that she once was. She revealed to me that the matter prompted a meeting among parents and siblings, and her father was alone in his stance. Her mother approved of our plan, and all her brothers were in support of it. Finding himself alone on this matter prompted Mr. Dadzie to soften his stance. From then on, we resumed regular communication. "Love never gives up, never loses faith, is always hopeful, and endures through every circumstance" (1 Cor. 13:7 NLT).

CHAPTER 16

THE RESET AND
THE TRIGGERS

"Every setback is a setup for a major comeback." —
Carley Montemuro

O n October 13, 2003, I was hit with a deadly blow as my mother passed away unexpectedly. Sylvia was gravely disappointed when I informed her. All she could say was, "Oh! Your Mum. I wanted to see her!" She would never get to know her would-be mother-in-law in person. This was something she tried to do just under five months prior but for her father's insistence. Suddenly, it had become eternally impossible. Sylvia was devastated. She asked to attend the funeral, but I discouraged her from making the trip and advised her to concentrate on her studies instead. I was also not in the right frame of mind as my mother's death had come so abruptly. Moreover, Sylvia and I were still working on keeping the relationship going, so I did not want it exposed to public eye. As yet, none of my relatives knew I was in a relationship, and I was happy to keep it at that level. Forty days after my mother's death, her funeral was held in November 2003.

149

I kept Sylvia apprised of all the preparations and the proceedings. She encouraged me throughout the entire time. Shortly afterwards, I picked up a teaching job in a high school sixty-seven miles away from home. On that note, we survived the year 2003. It was a year full of drama for me: it came with a bachelor's degree, mother's death, and a new job. Interestingly, Sylvia was to undergo a similar experience the following year.

In 2004, I got quite relaxed. God had revealed to me who my wife would be. We were already friends so I felt we needed no courtship. I believed that I did not necessarily have to know her further than I did at that moment. Further steps in this direction should be straight toward marriage, which I was not ready for as yet. I was afraid if we became more intimate in the name of knowing more about each other, new fears would result. In spite of my steely resolve, I was still not immune to sexual temptation. Sylvia could not be wrong for me so whatever baggage she came with, regardless of how adverse, marriage would still be in my interest. Sylvia was not only meant for me; I was also meant for her. That realization contributed to my relaxation in the relationship. I would not visit Sylvia for long periods of time. Even though we talked occasionally on the phone, I never brought up the subject of marriage. I visited her only at her request, and that made her worry about my seriousness.

Meanwhile, a number of suitors were coming forward to ask for Sylvia's hand in marriage. Her beauty caught the eyes of many would-be husbands. These were all well-to-do men compared to me, yet Sylvia felt nothing in her heart for them. She decided to be truthful to them and to herself. She told some of them point blank that she had no love for them. Some of them found it very heartbreaking while others could not take it. She felt deep in her heart and spirit that there was no way she could live in the future without me. She could not understand it, and for a moment, she thought she was under some sort of a spell. However, knowing my steadfastness in Christ Jesus and her own beliefs suggested something to the contrary. *Why then is he not coming forward when everybody else was?* She asked herself. She still felt very attracted to me, more than she felt toward anybody else regardless of the wealth they flaunted in her face. I was not privy to these details at that time, and Sylvia did not want me to know that I had rivals either. She really wanted me to come forward on my own, but I showed no sign to that effect. That was frustrating to a young lady with marriage ambitions.

At one point in time, Sylvia confided in our old friend, Blay-Nyanzu, who calmed her down with hopeful revelations about me and my promising future. That seemed to have settled her temporarily, but the pressure was still on. Sylvia still did not know what I knew, and I gave no reason for my relaxation in the relationship. While she expected the relationship to move to a higher gear, I was still applying the breaks. She did not want to put pressure on me either. Her eagerness and my relaxation, therefore, created an atmosphere of stress for her.

One evening when I was at home helping my nieces with their homework, Azay dropped a letter on me. As soon as I took it, I recognized the handwriting. It was from Sylvia. I quickly opened the letter and read. In it she stated that a woman, a family friend, came to see her parents on behalf of a gentleman who wanted to marry her. Sylvia's parents had informed her and would be requiring a response from her soon. Sylvia knew I was there and she needed to know my thoughts first before her parents contacted her officially. I knew she did not really mean it, because she already knew my thoughts, but I understood her position because for a long time, I had never talked to her about our future marriage. It was only rational that she assessed her chances. She would not want to lose out in case I had changed my mind. That was clearly a clever way of asking, "Would you come forward now or forget about me?" Sylvia was at her wit's best, something I admired her for. Knowing this, I penned a response to her the next day. I did not bite the bait. I was too mature to fall for her wits this time. I wrote to Sylvia that it was up to her to decide. She had known me, and I had made my intentions clear. I was not ready for marriage, but if she would wait for me, then she had my word. I stressed that since she was still waiting to finish her degree, I preferred that she concentrated on her academic studies and get her bachelor's degree like I had. Then, we could plan together to get the relationship to whichever level we wanted.

Nevertheless, that letter was a wake-up call for me. Before I concluded my letter, something struck me. I felt very sure within myself. I realized that Sylvia's letter was another way of inviting me to reaffirm my proposal. I remembered Sign #2 again. Sylvia's letter was another effort coming from her. The sign I considered most difficult to manifest was once again unfolding before me. It was being proven for the second time. "What a God I serve!" I exclaimed to myself. I was very grateful He had proved more than faithful. I knew I was not only reading a message from Sylvia but also one from our God who had always prompted Sylvia for my sake.

So, I inked in my conclusion, "You know it within your heart. Even if you marry someone else, we would still be the best of friends, and you will eventually end up with me still." How prophetic that was! Sylvia wrote back telling me she felt exactly the same way. In her words, I wrote her exact feelings at that time. Sylvia felt that even if she was offered the world without me, her life would still not be complete until she came back. She had never felt happier with any other man than her father. But now, the joy of having me as a future husband somehow overtook the joy she had with her father. She had needed me to reassure her of this potential joy. It was something she could not explain, but her heart absolutely loved the idea. I arranged to visit her on campus in a fortnight.

During that visit, we made planning our future marriage the priority of our agenda. I assured Sylvia of my unflinching stance. My only concerns were that I was not yet fully prepared, and she was still in school—everything pointed to the fact that we had to wait. Since Sylvia still had an Exchange Program to complete for her bachelor's, it was better to wait until after that. I urged her to avoid any marriage traps until she had finally graduated. Marriage comes with responsibilities, and she could not afford during that critical time of her final year to add more responsibilities to her already academically stressed life. I believed she might not be able to handle all that. Now she had an answer ready for whoever came forward. She would tell her parents she would finish school first before making any marriage decisions.

By the time she finished, we would be close to that decision. Sylvia felt very comforted by my submission and sided with me. It worked for us. I was thinking about her future, and she loved the idea that I was not that selfish. She loved it most when I told her I wanted her to have the same degree I had before we went into marriage; we would then be marrying as academic equals. I wanted her to have what I had and that resounded with her perfectly. Sylvia was exceptionally glad about my visit. I knew this because she asked me when I would be returning for my next visit. This was the first time she had asked me for another visit in the midst of a current one.

We started to work on getting the relationship to a higher level as Sylvia neared her course completion. I had been introduced to her parents, brothers, and a few other family members. Gradually, Sylvia and I were coming out into the open with our relationship despite our initial unwillingness to do so. We just could not hide some things from her family anymore. Once her parents acknowledged us, we could no longer hide. In early spring 2004, Sylvia had finished the theoretical aspect of her studies.

While she was waiting to begin an exchange program as a course requirement for her bachelor's degree, Sylvia went back to her alma mater to teach as an intern. I was quite impressed when I heard that she had gotten that opportunity. Wesley Girls' High School was arguably the most elite and prestigious girls' high school in the region. So, for Sylvia to get the opportunity to teach in such a school meant a great deal to me. It told me about her diligence, and I could not have been prouder. Once she told me about it, I planned to surprise her. I promised to visit her a week after she moved to one of the teachers' apartments on campus. I advised her to leave her bulky stuff behind in Winneba and proceed with the basic things she would need. There would be opportunity for her to bring her other belongings after she had fairly assessed life's situation in her new abode.

In reality, however, I intended to help her go get her belongings when I visited. I did not tell her I would be coming in my father's Mercedes Benz sedan. Before, I had always visited her by public transportation except when she was in Kumasi on a visit to her father. On the eve of the appointed day, I went for my father's car in the evening. I thoroughly polished it inside and out. Early the following day, I set out on the over 135-mile (215 km) journey. I only told Sylvia I was on my way when I made a rest stop. I went straight to the visitors car park when I arrived at the school. I called her to come and take me to her new apartment as that was my first time ever visiting the school. I still had the car's tinted windows rolled up when I saw her pop up from the northwestern corner of the car park. I observed as she looked around with no sight of me. She called my phone to confirm whether I was indeed, at the car park. I answered that I was, but she could still not find me. "I can see you, so how come you don't see me?" I teased. She dropped her hands as if she had lost confidence of ever finding me. I told her I was standing behind a black Mercedes-Benz sedan. She looked around and found it. She turned toward the direction of the car but walked desperately to it as there was no sign of a person near it. I had already opened the door slightly. As she walked round the vehicle to my side, I quickly pushed open the door and shot out like a bullet. She screamed with her hands in the air like a surrendering prisoner of war. It took some seconds for her to calm her nerves before I could give her a hug. I invited her to get in the car and direct me while we drove to her apartment.

We were both happy as Sylvia had started a completely independent life. She had a decent apartment, not so plush but not bad for a beginner either. She cooked while we chatted. After our meal, Sylvia took me to another apartment to introduce me to another nice young man who was also a new teacher in the school. His name was Kwesi Essien. He had been nice to her, and they had become friends already. I took the opportunity to engage him in a chat for a short time before we went back to Sylvia's apartment. In the afternoon, we drove to Winneba to get the rest of her belongings that she could not bring along earlier.

On arrival, I did something that both stunned and mesmerized Sylvia. Her house had an open court with a wide gate. I decided to enter and park the sedan inside to make it easier for us to pack her belongings into it. However, there was a ramp at the gate with a sharp drop on the inside for the court of the house was set in a depression. This caused the bottom of the car, specifically under the engine compartment, to screech at the apex of the ramp as I went in slowly. Sylvia became alarmed and asked me to park outside. I looked at her and calmly asked her to be patient while I tried another maneuver. After years of driving, I had had more experience in dealing with such situations. I put the car in reverse gear and came off the ramp. I then turned it around in a three-point turn to enter the gate in the reverse gear. Since there was no load in the trunk, there was more height at the back axle than the front, which was weighed down by the heavy engine. I descended backwards into the house slowly and smoothly. As the back axle went down the ramp, the car slanted backward giving less weight and a lift to the front. In this manner, I gently came off the ramp successfully, descending smoothly into the courtyard. I came to a stop in the middle of the courtyard having parked at a space near the door to her room. With the look of surprise in Sylvia's eyes, a smile of satisfaction in her face and a loud laughter, I knew I had made her proud. Mrs. Dadzie could not hide her joy when she saw her daughter and myself emerge from the car. That in itself made a big statement. I knew I was then acknowledged in the family. This was the second time I was meeting Mrs. Dadzie and the first time since the perturbation with Mr. Dadzie. I understood Mrs. Dadzie was glad that I still found faith in her daughter even in the face of a challenge that threatened our relationship. Mr. Dadzie was, however, absent as always. Once again, he was busy in Kumasi.

Mrs. Dadzie cooked for us after which we stuffed Sylvia's belongings into the car. Mrs. Dadzie bid us goodbye as we slowly made it for the gate. I could sense Sylvia's voice resound with great joy. She waved back to her proud mother as we made our way out of the gate. This time we had no problem with the ramp at the gate because we left in the same manner as we came in. Before we departed the Winneba township, we paid a brief visit to our old friend, Blay-Nyanzu, to see how he was faring. He was very glad to see us together. He gave a smile of satisfaction and felt vindicated. If he painted a promising picture of my future to Sylvia when she found the going tough and had confided in him, this was the proof of things to come.

We headed back to Cape Coast, to the campus of Wesley Girls High School. We unpacked Sylvia's stuff while Kwesi Essien, the other young teacher, came to help. We sat indoors for most of the rest of the time. Sylvia and I were both quite satisfied with the way things were unraveling. She told me how her father was gradually coming around after knowing a little more about me and how her siblings and mother were all in agreement with our friendship and possible union. It was getting late when I asked to leave. When Sylvia asked me to sleep over, I refused politely citing integrity as the main reason. She was sad I did not stay for the night, but she was totally on board with me. I explained to Sylvia that even though both of us meant well, it was more prudent to avoid traps than try to survive them. I drove off to the nearby campus of the University of Cape Coast to find accommodation. Blay-Nyanzu called to find out if we had arrived. He was also happy that I did not stay overnight in Sylvia's apartment. He was not surprised either by my decision as he was well acquainted with my penchant for integrity.

The following morning, I drove back to Sylvia's apartment. We took breakfast together after which I dropped her off at the Staff Common Room. Prior to that, I had thought of something creative in order to leave her a lasting thought long after I was gone. As Sylvia got out of the car and walked toward the door, I watched her till she was about to enter the building. Then, I called her back as if she had left something inside the car. She made a quick turn and came back to the car. As she neared, I lowered the windows even further down and whispered to her, "I love you." She broke out loud in a hearty laughter as she made her way back to the staffroom door again, her feet rather wobbly as if my words were intoxicating. Indeed, for the first time since our acquaintance, she had heard the word *love* out of my mouth, however causal it was. Previously, I had consciously used the word 'like' instead, as that word safely had no sexual connotations attached. She held the door post with her left hand and turned to my direction. She waved at me, still drenched in laughter while I slowly drove off. "*Now, that's a lasting impression,*" I surmised.

A few weeks after my historic visit, Sylvia called me in a sad tone. I realized all was not well with her. It was her turn for bereavement and my time to encourage her. One of her aunties who had traveled to Maryland from Ghana on vacation had passed away before she could return. Sylvia called to inform me of it. She sounded devastated on the other end of the line. For a couple of weeks, I kept talking to her on the phone, getting updates and encouraging her.

At last, the date for the funeral was fixed and Sylvia informed me. I realized she expected me to attend, but I was not sure how I was going to be introduced. I felt uncomfortable about it, but I did not want to leave Sylvia alone in her time of mourning either. Other members of her extended family would be present. I was only known by a few people in her family. Attending this funeral would blow the lid completely off our relationship. I still thought it was too early to further expose our relationship, so I picked the phone and consulted Blay-Nyanzu. He advised me to show up as that was also an opportunity to make a statement of my future desire. He concluded that he would be there himself, so we could keep each other company. That was a welcome relief for me. In the afternoon of the eve of the funeral, I set out for Winneba. I called on Blay-Nyanzu at his hostel. He took me to a spot to have some malt drinks before proceeding to Sylvia's house in the evening. She was obviously happy to see me as her movements suddenly quickened upon seeing us.

The wake was to continue overnight as mourners and well-wishers trooped in at various times. Nyanzu and I sat before a console that blared out music through loud speakers. We kept changing CD upon CD. Sylvia joined us briefly to welcome us. She went back to her busy schedule and returned from time to time. Shortly before midnight, sympathizers stopped coming by, and the traffic didn't resume until the dawn of the next day. Everyone in the house retired indoors. I was left alone at the console as I refused Sylvia's plea to take a rest indoors. *It is time to show strength and resilience,* I thought to myself. Sylvia came to me from time to time to see how I was faring in the middle of the night and in the middle of the open court of the house. At about 4:30 A.M. when life begun to resuscitate in the house, Sylvia and Blay-Nyanzu came up to me and pleaded with me one more time to at least take a nap before daybreak, as I had sat awake all through the night. It was going to be another day full of activities. I got up and threw myself into one of the rooms to relax.

During the day, I stayed with Blay-Nyanzu and Kwesi Essien, who had also arrived from Wesley Girl's High School that morning for the funeral. I mostly shied away from the family as I still wanted to keep myself as hidden as I possibly could. I stood outside the Winneba Methodist Church with Blay-Nyanzu and Kwesi Essien as Sylvia's family members gathered inside. I heard Sylvia's voice speaking in a tribute to her deceased aunt. Gradually, her voice shook, and I realized she was in tears as she spoke with a sobbing voice toward the end. *Oh, poor Sylvia! And I am not close enough to give you my shoulder,* I said to myself. I bought an audio CD of selected gospel music from a nearby store when the church ceremony was over and the body was carried to the cemetery.

When we went back to the house. I took to the console again. I put in my new CD which played the most loved gospels for all who had come to the funeral. In the late afternoon, Kwesi and I went to Sylvia and asked to leave. While Kwesi was returning to Cape Coast, I was going back to Kumasi. I had a long journey ahead of me. Blay-Nyanzu saw us off as Sylvia could not go far with us because the funeral was still in progress.

A couple of months after my return to Kumasi, I made a personal trip to Mr. Dadzie at his Kumasi abode in a Geo Prism sedan belonging to Sister Pat. I parked a distance away and walked more than four blocks to his place of residence. I wanted Mr Dadzie to see me as who I really was, not to have him think that his daughter's future husband came from a well-to-do family. I also did not want him to think that I came to show off. I knew I would lose access to the cars if I left Azay's home, something that would happen eventually. Mr Dadzie welcomed me, and I officially informed him of my interest in his daughter.

This was not the customary way of doing this sort of thing, but mine was not an ordinary thing. I was motivated by the evidence of God's hand to pursue everything that I thought good for the marriage without much regard to the cultural norms. I was emboldened to carry things out myself and not pay too much attention to people, customs, and traditions. Prayer was my main weapon. I prayed, and I pursued. It always worked. As we would see later, customs and traditions gave way to me. Mr. Dadzie replied that he was aware that we were friends, but he would still have to find out from his daughter if she consented to my proposal. He concluded that whatever she said, he would let me know. He was not to go to Winneba until the following month, but I was not worried. I knew the answer would be nothing but positive.

When I begged leave of him, Mr. Dadzie took me out and saw me off as far as the bus station. I could no longer hide the fact that I drove as he wanted to see me off to the point of boarding a bus before bidding me goodbye. I then revealed to him that I came with a vehicle, and we walked to the car. I felt bad letting him walk all that distance back to his house alone. Mr. Dadzie was not worried, but I begged him to get in the car and let me take him back home because, apart from the long distance, the night had also fallen. I dropped Mr. Dadzie in front of his abode and drove back home. At the appointed time, I went back to find out the result from Mr. Dadzie as courtesy demanded. The smile on his face rather foreshadowed a good response. He told me that Sylvia consented and that she was happy I came to see him about her. I then took the opportunity to shower praise on his daughter for her unique ability, discipline, and love for the Word of God. I also thanked him for bringing her up in the way she had grown. I told him more about myself and the fact that I stayed with my cousin and his family. I also revealed to him where I lived and where my parents lived. He was sad to hear that my mother was no more. He offered a little word of advice, and he saw me off.

Chapter 17

The "Knocking" And The Graduation

"The starting point of all achievements is desire." —
Napoleon Hill

In the middle of June 2004, Sylvia came to Kumasi to visit her father and obviously to see me. It was her last visit before she left for her year abroad program. She mostly spent the day with me, while I dropped her off at her father's abode in the late afternoon. For the entire period that she remained in Kumasi, Sylvia jostled between the two of us on a daily basis. When I picked her up in the morning on the first day, we took a route that passed in front of a middle school where Osei Moses, one of my close friends, taught. This friend of mine has remained loyal since we first met in high school. Naturally, I felt obliged to stop by and introduce Sylvia to him. Years later, as fate would have it, Moses would be very instrumental in our decision to move to the United States. From the middle school, I took Sylvia to see Akos, the younger of my two sisters. This sister of mine happened to be the only one in whom I would confide concerning the relationship. She was the only one who had prior knowledge that I even intended to marry. I asked her to keep whatever she saw and heard secret. If she observed anything worth talking about, she would discuss it with me and me only. Within a week, Sylvia was back in Winneba.

Two weeks later, I paid her what I thought would be my last visit to her before she departed for her exchange program abroad. Nevertheless, that visit turned out not to be the last one. Sylvia told me the program had been scheduled to take place in the Republic of Benin. Then, she dazed me with a question, "Will you give me a promise ring?" She requested. "A promise ring? What's that?" I asked. Indeed, until this moment, I never knew anything like that existed. A wedding ring I knew but I had never heard of a promise ring. So, I probed for more explanation. Sylvia told me a promise ring was a type of ring ladies wear on their middle finger to show would-be suitors that they are already lined up with somebody, even though they are not married yet. "I see," I responded in almost a sigh. That was news to me, so I asked her to describe how promise rings look like. To keep it simple, Sylvia asked me to go to the jeweler's and ask him or her to show me the different kinds of promise rings they had; then, I would be able to choose from a variety. I agreed and promised to try when I got back. I managed to get her a promise ring a few days later. I was not sure how Sylvia would like it, but when I showed it to her, she was very appreciative and felt so proud about it. After a week, she left Ghana for the Republic of Benin. We kept communicating through both e-mail and snail mail. I called her but seldom. She would tell me about the challenges she faced over there. I would give advice as best as I could. While her letters arrived in paragraphs, I replied in pages. Life went on this way until the first quarter of the year 2005 when I hatched a plan. I wanted to surprise her by initiating major steps toward marriage before she arrived.

One day, I visited Mr. Dadzie in his Kumasi abode and told him I wanted to perform the "knocking" ceremony. According to the tradition of our land, the knocking ceremony was the first step toward marriage. It signifies the man's attempt to literally enter the home of the young lady; hence the term, *knocking*. The knocking ceremony is the first opportunity for the significant relatives on both sides to officially acquaint themselves with one another. The gentleman would inform his parents of his desire for a woman he had seen. Then, he would ask his parents to go and officially solicit the hand of the lady for him. Usually, the man's parents would ask him to lead them to the lady's house. The lady's parents would welcome them and ask of their mission. When the parents have communicated their son's intention to the lady's parents, they would present a token and a gift to the lady's parents. Then, the lady's parents would ask them to leave while they consulted with their daughter to find out if she consented and also to seek the advice of other relevant relatives. Traditionally, the lady's family would send an emissary to investigate the man's background as well. Another day would be scheduled for the gentleman's parents to return for the response. Rarely, the lady would be called to meet her possible in-laws. It was normally the second time when the gentleman's parents came for the feedback that the lady is officially brought to meet with her would-be in-laws and husband. If the lady happened not to consent, she might not see them at all. Such was and still is the prevailing custom.

However, I took it upon myself to solely negotiate the curves of custom and traditions unconventionally. Upon hearing my mission, Mr. Dadzie asked me to come back another time for the response. As usual, he had to consult his wife and other significant family members in Winneba for their consent as well as to determine when and where the ceremony would be performed. On that note I left, and Mr. Dadzie saw me off.

Two weeks later, I went back to see Mr. Dadzie. Here is a man who put reason beyond tripping traditions. Tradition dictated that such ceremonies took place in the young lady's house in the presence of all her parents. Since Mr. Dadzie and I were in Kumasi, he made it more convenient by wrestling consent from the relevant family authorities in Winneba to hold the ceremony in Kumasi against the traditional norm. I would violate tradition on an even bigger scale come that day. Customarily, such a trip included the suitor himself and his two parents or their representatives. Neither of my parents was involved. My mother was no more, even though she had a successor. I did not inform my father either, because of something that had happened the previous year. To cut a long story short, his impressions about my possible future marriage amounted to literally pouring cold water on my warm hands. From that day on, I vowed to black him out on all matters concerning my marriage. I only informed him when I was done with my marriage preparation. To me, ours was not anybody's average marriage. It was a marriage arranged by God Himself, and I would not permit any man in whatever capacity to discourage me, hijack or pervert the proceedings.

On the appointed day, I substituted my father with one of my maternal uncles named Brenya. I also took along my elder brother and younger sister, Emmanuel and Akos respectively. Before we set out, I made them swear an oath not to divulge any information regarding what we were going to do. With that agreement, we went in Sister Pat's silver sedan. It was a short ceremony in which Mr. Dadzie and a cousin of Sylvia's represented her family. My uncle spoke on my behalf, introducing each of us as custom demanded. Mr. Dadzie also introduced himself and Sylvia's cousin. Then, my uncle told of our mission and reiterated that as Christians we did not endorse alcoholism; hence we presented a token in place of hard drinks. Mr. Dadzie could not agree more, emphasizing that as a fellow Christian, he would like everything to be conducted in a godly manner. Mr. Dadzie urged us to uphold that principle in all the ceremonies that would attend the wedding. He thanked us and accepted the gift on behalf of the family, stating that he would inform his daughter and his family about this and would let me know the outcome. My uncle then got up and thanked Mr. Dadzie for their warm reception. He then asked leave on our behalf. We shook hands, and that concluded the ceremony. As we departed, I emphasized the need for all who attended with me to keep everything secret unto the wedding day. I was glad I had moved a step closer as Sylvia would then see concrete evidence that her marriage was gradually cooking.

When I went home and reflected upon my marriage preparations so far, I was surprised how I'd pulled this off and avoided all the traditional procedures in order to keep it secret. Money? I had none, but I had succeeded. Then, I remembered God's Word, "With God, everything is possible" (Matthew 19:26 NLT). I felt very grateful. Sylvia was away in another country and everything was being done through her father. It took a couple of days for her to receive the news. I could have called her instantly and made her aware, but it was traditionally the father's prerogative to break such news to his daughter. It also provided the father the opportunity to further interrogate his daughter to see if her consent was still intact before the would-be husband's intentions progressed further. So, I restrained myself until Sylvia's father had broken the news to her. Her joy knew no bounds when she heard it. At long last, her one and only Aaron was making the big moves she had long awaited.

At the end of the knocking stage, the lady is legally regarded as a wife even though the would-be couple cannot consummate the relationship until after the actual marriage ceremony. This is the betrothal stage, and it could still be long before the marriage ceremony itself took place. Due to the influence of Western culture nowadays, many people erroneously refer to the traditional marriage as the engagement and the wedding as the marriage. In fact, the next step following a successful knocking is the traditional, customary marriage ceremony, which is the actual marriage. After this stage, the couple can live together legally as husband and wife. The civil or church wedding ceremony is optional once the traditional ceremony has been performed. Civil or church wedding constitutes a recent addition from Western culture and Christianity.

Although Sylvia was away in another country, she was effectively regarded as my wife from then on. After a successful knocking, custom demands that the father of the bride consults the stakeholders and furnishes the groom with a list of the items he demands for the dowry during the marriage ceremony. Before we left the knocking ceremony, Mr. Dadzie called me aside and whispered to me that he would call me to come for the list when he had gone to see his wife and family.

From then on, I prayed that Mr. Dadzie would not factor his daughter's beauty into the calculation or else I would have to pay a fortune. He called me after a few weeks, and I inquired nervously about the list. It was fairly modest. Mr. Dadzie was careful not to burden me with too much cost, which might, in turn, adversely affect our initial financial position after marriage. He also did not want to make it too easy for me as that might also reflect on the respect for his daughter. He found a compromise in the middle, which I found very reasonable.

However, four days after I got the list and studied it, I returned to Mr. Dadzie with a modification request. I found out that a sewing machine, which was a traditional requirement for all dowries, was among the items listed. I reasoned that in this modern age, the idea of including sewing machine had outlived its purpose. Instead, a personal computer would be more appropriate as that would reflect modernity. I had my doubts that a man as principled as Mr. Dadzie would budge, but that did not stop me from trying either. True to my assumption, he rejected my idea stating that a sewing machine was included for a traditional purpose and that the list was carefully thought out. Any modification meant that he would have to go back to consult with Mrs. Dadzie and, at least, Sylvia's Uncle John. "If you want to buy a computer for her, you are welcome to do so at any time. Avoid choices that may complicate issues for you and further delay my daughter's marriage. I have held up both of you long enough. Once you are ready, take a straight path and keep it simple," he advised. I realized that Mr. Dadzie was right, because computers were certainly more expensive and would have added additional costs to the dowry. On that note, I thanked him and left for home.

Months later, Sylvia returned from her exchange program to prepare for graduation. She called me on the day of her arrival to announce her presence back on the soil of Ghana. I called back in the late evening and promised to come over to officially welcome her. I also took the opportunity to talk to Mr. Dadzie who had earlier traveled to Winneba in anticipation of his daughter's return.

A week later, I went to visit Sylvia. It had been a year since we last saw each other, and she was very happy to see me. I wanted us to stay outdoors as usual, but knowing the sensitivity of the subject she had in mind for discussion, Sylvia suggested we go indoors for privacy. I was both curious and cautious as to what she had up her sleeve. Slowly, I followed her to her room, hoping she would not do anything abominable. I sat in a chair while she sat on her bed facing in the opposite direction. She was always at her usual smiling best. With her gracefulness and her countenance so lovely, Sylvia's voice was as melodious as I could ever have imagined. We spent most of the time in her room chatting. She only left to bring us food or drink. We spoke a lot about her experiences in the Republic of Benin, her studies, thesis, impending graduation, new acquaintances she made during the period, and so on. I was still shy, so I kept a low voice. However, Sylvia laughed aloud intermittently whenever she got excited about anything. We also talked about the rest of the procedures in the marriage process.

Then came the reason why Sylvia wanted our conversation to be so private. She got more intimate and threw a question at me that caught me off balance. "So, how many children would you

want me to give you?" she asked. I could not say anything immediately. I sat back, and she started laughing. She realized that I had
not thought about it. "Girls are always two steps ahead, you know?"
she added. I said I needed a boy and a girl. She looked at me closely
with a wide smile and said in a low voice, "God willing, I would
give you an extra one for a bonus. How about that?" I succumbed.

Now that she was back from her exchange program, Sylvia
expected to be confirmed as a tutor by her alma mater, Wesley Girls'
High School, where she previously did her internship. However,
they would not. Unbeknownst to her, a rival school, Holy Child
High School, had heard of the exploits of a sleek, young female
French tutor at Wesley Girl's High School and had been scouting
for her even before she went abroad. Holy Child and Wesley Girls
were and still are both unisex, prestigious, and the two most competitive girls' schools in the region if not the country. They rivaled
each other in every way imaginable. Holy Child High School had
finished an elaborate arrangement to entice Sylvia into their midst.
They had already secured a fully furnished, two-bedroom apartment as part of her package with other perks. Thus, Sylvia was
wooed to this school to teach French. She was to be appointed a
House Mistress for one of the dormitories a year later. I visited
her a couple of times in her new apartment. A few months later, in
the last quarter of 2005, I attended her graduation ceremony at the
campus of the University College of Winneba. From there, it was
game on. The pressure was on me. Now that Sylvia had obtained
the bachelor's degree I wanted her to have before marriage, the
onus was on me to set the marriage wheels turning. It was a her-
culean task for me. I never expected to get to this level that fast.

Anyone who is familiar with traditional African settings can
testify to the fact that going into marriage involves a lot of things,
people, customs, and elaborate procedures. The families of both
sides from the first generation to the last are involved. That was
a problem for me, because I did not want many people vested

in my marriage. I felt if I followed tradition and allowed that to happen, Sylvia and I might not have absolute control over our marriage. Therefore, keeping our arrangements as low key as possible became my preoccupation. People who knew my preparations were absolutely few in number. Keeping our planning at that level of secrecy was highly contrary to the prevailing tradition. And, flouting the customs for personal expediency was never an easy thing to do. There would certainly be a backlash. I kept praying while I proceeded from one step to another. I also kept Sylvia in the dark as to the notion of keeping my side of the deal as secret as possible. I did not want her to ask me why or assume that my people might be evil. So, not only did I have to keep my marriage plans secret, I also had to keep the knowledge of the secrecy from my would-be wife.

It was a very difficult and dicey situation. My main reason was that if God truly had led me well in the past and was still leading me in the marriage process, why allow the customs and traditions of man to dictate proceedings instead of keeping it pure and sanctified? I believed He had started it and being God as He is, He was capable of seeing us through to the end regardless of customs and traditions.

Again, with the rumors and misconceptions between our two ethnic groups, it was very easy for mistrust to slip into our marriage or even discourage me altogether if I allowed many people to have knowledge about my marriage plans. I did not want to create the grounds for anybody to sow seeds of mistrust in my mind. I absolutely relied on God and hoped He would help me pull through the same way He did during the knocking stage. All these called for a lot of thinking, planning, scheming, and praying. Above all, I had faith in God that I would succeed, hence I persevered. Fortunately, because I lived in Azay's house, I was isolated from the extended family so my movements could not be tracked. One preparation after another, I fulfilled almost everything under the radar.

Sylvia at her bachelor's degree graduation.

A week after her graduation, Sylvia visited her father in Kumasi. She had hoped that soon after her graduation, we would tie the knot. So, she took the opportunity to come to me for us to discuss the way forward, hoping to set a date for our wedding somewhere before the end of 2005. After assessing my preparation and my financial situation, I declared that I was not yet ready. I, therefore, advised

Sylvia that we should not fix a date just then. Putting her off broke her heart, and she came to tears. I was very sad seeing tears run down her cheeks. It was a low point for me, but I would not budge. I felt it was good to break her heart at this stage in order to fix it later than to pretend all was well only to discover later that all was not well. That would be irrecoverable. I consoled and assured her that I was ready but I was expecting to rev up my savings to a higher level instead of the current amount I had. It made sense because we never knew what would follow after the wedding. No matter what followed, we should be able to foot all the bills subsequent to the wedding ourselves. Since I never wanted to borrow for my wedding expenses, I did not expect anybody to invest heavily in it either. It was, therefore, critical that I saved not just enough for the wedding but also that I had a surplus to take care of contingent liabilities subsequent to our marriage. This was going to be one long journey for which we needed to prepare not just adequately but abundantly well. Sylvia understood but could not bring herself to deal with the uncertainties of tomorrow. She had been patient and had waited for years already. She needed a range of time at least. Consequently, I told her my estimation was a date in the first half of the following year. That, I was sure of, but we should wait until we felt we were ready to marry the next day before fixing a date. On that note, we rested our marriage discussions and Sylvia went back to Winneba.

Chapter 18

Marriage Preparation

Enthusiasm is the baking powder of life.
—Marie Fontaine

Fortunately for me, the financial boost I was expecting came in less than a month after Sylvia left. I called her to tell her that I would be coming to Winneba for us to set up a date for our marriage in about a week's time. Meanwhile, we had to devote ourselves to prayer and fasting in order to ensure our timing coincided with God's. Sylvia was ecstatic to hear the news and could not wait for that day to come. I went to visit her as promised, and we set the date for Saturday, February 11, 2006. We had already entered the month of November, 2005.

Fixing a date was no easy task. No matter how long we waited, I still did not feel my preparation was complete. There was always something left that I needed to put in place. Even on the day of our wedding, I still did not feel I had prepared adequately. I have a word of advice for would-be couples on marriage preparation at the end of this book on this issue. In the following month, Sylvia visited me in Kumasi to follow up on matters we had discussed the previous month. The first thing she did was to offer me two hundred US dollars to help me financially. At first, I was reluctant to accept her contribution because culturally it was not acceptable. According to African tradition, the man bore all the costs of the dowry and any item pertinent to the marriage necessary to prove his financial and logistical adequacy needed to start and cater for a family. Sylvia realized my reluctance but urged me to take the money. "This is my contribution toward our marriage. Forget about tradition. We are in Christ; hence we are a new creation. We must bear one another's burden as in Galatians 6:2, you know? This is from my heart. I can't leave you to bear all the burden," she insisted. She explained that since the last time we met when we could not set a date, she had been thinking of what she could do to help me. She, therefore, took the money from her savings. I was overwhelmed by her having such sympathy. I was completely humbled. I took the money and could not have been more appreciative. Once again, Sylvia had demonstrated to me beyond a doubt that she was the ideal woman for me.

If this is the woman I was going to marry, then God gave me a helper indeed. She would go to every length to seek my welfare, so why not die for her? I thought to myself. The money involved was not much but that was not important to me. What made a big impression on me was the thought behind it—Sylvia's willingness to share my burden in whatever way she could. Moreover, choosing to save in the more stable US. dollars in a country where the Ghanaian Cedi was the currency made a big statement to me about Sylvia's wisdom and foresight. I vowed that I would be the best of husbands for her sake. I would do whatever would lie in my power as a husband to make her happy and even more progressive. To me, Sylvia typified the woman in Proverbs: "House and riches are the inheritance of fathers; and a prudent wife is from the Lord" (Prov. 19:14 KJV)

Sylvia and I had already been talking about how we envisioned the wedding would be. However, we had not comprehensively reviewed it in detail until this day when we started putting pen to paper. We all agreed to a modest ceremony without much fanfare. We planned to do the traditional marriage as custom demanded, but it would be followed by a Christian wedding in church the same day. The wedding would also be followed by a reception right from the chapel. The following day being Sunday, we planned to have a special lunch after church service. Sylvia's Uncle John had been a role model for her family, and we wanted to honor him by inviting him to chair the function for both the reception and the lunch. Sylvia was to convey the message to him when she went back. We also considered other pertinent issues such as the protocol team, the gift table team, the wedding hymns, food, and drinks, video and photography among other tasks. Having thus planned everything, Sylvia departed for Winneba to see her parents and talk over our preparations with them.

Sylvia and I kept on talking and praying while we moved ahead with our plans to ensure the success of the marriage. In late December 2005, I visited Sylvia at Winneba as she needed to introduce me to her church and some of the dignitaries in her family before the marriage day. I left very early that morning knowing what lay ahead of us for the day. I also needed to return to Kumasi that same day. After we made some introduction rounds, we returned to Sylvia's house for a late lunch after which we decided to go to the beach to cool off and further discuss our preparations for the wedding. We specifically wanted to discuss the order of the service and the design of the invitations. As soon as I arrived back in Kumasi, I was going to send the design to the printer and send Sylvia the bulk of the cards for distribution. Luckily, my brother, Abraham, had offered to pay for the invitation cards.

While we were still at the beach, Uncle John, who had been slated to chair our functions, came from Accra to the Dadzies' home.

He had a message for us. When he was told we had departed to the beach, he followed us there and took a seat right in front of us. He informed us that he would be attending a conference in Europe as a representative of the Forestry Department, a governmental agency he headed. The date for the conference fell in the very week when we planned to have our wedding. So, it was impossible for him to attend. However, this was also a wedding for his beloved niece, and he did not want to miss. Consequently, he pleaded with us to shift the date forward, if possible, to enable him to attend the conference and still be present to witness our wedding ceremony, chair our functions and provide any other help we may need with his presence. Sylvia's face changed all of a sudden. That was the last thing she had expected. She had already suffered enough waiting to get this date and was ready to go. She could not wait a minute longer. I turned to her with a smile and calmness of spirit, a technique that forced her to relax. I asked her to allow us to accept and jointly find a date in March by which time Uncle John would have returned from his conference in Europe. Slowly, Sylvia nodded as if a rope had been tied to her head thus preventing her from bringing it down for the nodding. I told Uncle John that we would inform him when we settled on a later date. Uncle John thanked us for our understanding and begged leave of us after that.

As soon as he left, we set about setting another date in place of the February 11, 2006. I would not have minded even if it went to the middle of the year, but Sylvia would not allow the first Saturday of March 2006 to pass without having the wedding ring slipped onto her finger. I sympathized with her, so we chose March 04, 2006 for both the customary marriage ceremony and the church wedding. We revised our plans accordingly and left for her house afterwards. Sylvia had still not come to terms with the new development but I was all for it because it gave me extra preparation time. I could also draw one more salary before the wedding. I thought having extra liquidity is always good for such occasions.

As I have already indicated, marriage in the traditional sense was and still is something very sensitive and extensive. It involved the entire families of the bride and the groom from the first generation to the last. All manner of solicitations and agreements are sought to ensure the security and stability of the union. Contemporarily, customary marriage is compounded with a western style wedding in the church. That was the situation we faced. However, I wanted to limit the customary part and simplify the wedding aspect as best I could. I aimed at limiting the number of people involved to the minimum, at least from my side. I wanted a very low-key ceremony, without much publicity, if possible.

As the wedding day drew near, I reviewed all the customary procedures. Going against the traditional norm, I eliminated any procedure that required too many people. I concentrated on those traditions that went to the core of the marriage process. I tried to keep the message from going out too far. I made sure that only a few people knew of my marriage and my preparations. I confided in Lucy, Abraham's wife, whenever I did not know what to expect from Sylvia's side, mainly because she had been there before. By the grace of God, I had succeeded to this point without much publicity. This was exactly how I wanted it. I prayed to God to grant me the grace and favor to continue onward in the same manner. To my astonishment, He did. For instance, by the end of December 2005, I had informed my church of my desire to marry. It was the practice of the church to require would-be couples to appear before a marriage committee for counseling six months prior if the church would sanction any marriage. However, I informed the church with less than three months remaining until the time of the wedding. It was risky, but I believed God was in this and as such nothing could derail us. The church could either ask us to postpone the date or refuse to have a hand in it if we objected. However, they reasoned with me and held a few counseling sessions both with me alone and together with Sylvia at various times within the next two months.

Our counseling was short, but we considered it most effective due to the pertinent and voluminous amount of counsel we received within that condensed time period. Usually, a marriage committee counseling session was presided over by two or three members, but in our case, almost every member of the marriage committee was summoned to attend our sessions. Mrs. Owusu Ansah, my pastor's wife, chaired the last day of the sessions. Each committee member would handle a topic or two. If the last day was particularly overwhelming for me, Sylvia was completely shocked due to the amount of details they went into with regard to sexual intimacy between couples. We were not prepared for that at all. I was green but Sylvia was even greener.

We thought (as a church) they would not go into much detail on sexual relations between husband and wife. We were wrong. Particularly when it came to the turn of Mrs. Owusu Ansah, it was a "No Holds Barred" session. She went into greater details unreservedly. I felt very shy and wanted her to cut things short so I could get out of there. Sylvia was not a quiet girl, but she was exceptionally quiet and motionless during that session. That is when I realized that she was completely overwhelmed. At that meeting, Sylvia was posed a question about sex and her answer made the panel burst into loud and hearty laughter. Her innocent answer gave her away as a virgin, and the panel confirmed it.

To me, that was significant because it was a further confirmation of Sign #3 in my covenant. If my previous assessment of Sylvia's virginity was inadequate, this was God providing the concrete proof I sought. The committee had no idea how their question, Sylvia's answer, and the subsequent laughter aided me in this regard. After that session, we went back home and discussed most of the revelations raised at the session about which we had no clue until then. It was quite revealing.

That evening was the first time we discussed bedroom matters ever since we first met over a decade ago. The counseling sessions had opened our eyes to certain matters about both manhood and womanhood. It was obvious we were inevitably getting there, and we had questions for each other. Frankly, I wanted to shy away from it in the beginning but Sylvia's curiosity knew no bounds now that our eyes were opened to intimate marital affairs. She kept asking me one intimate question after another. At last, I also started raining questions on her. I felt that if she was not that shy at this time to question me so intimately, why should I hide my own curiosity? We made sure we understood each other's point of view and sensed each other's sentiments about them.

After several hours of interaction, I bid her sound sleep while I went to my room to retire to bed for the night. When we met early the following morning, Sylvia still had questions for me. I knew the marriage counseling had generated a lot of excitement in her. I had never seen her so eager about marriage. Sylvia felt this was the time when she needed to know everything there was to know about me and my thoughts in order to prepare before things took her by surprise. Like I did, she also realized that she had a lot of preparations to make for me if our relationship were ever to blossom. It was important, therefore, that she knew my mindset and left nothing uncertain.

Later, after our marriage, Sylvia confessed that the counseling sessions had been very beneficial to her. Now, she remembers that session with fondness. Any time I talk about my pastor, she recalls his wife and the last counseling session. Indeed, the information we had was vital for our marriage. I am very grateful for the marriage committee's indispensable contribution. Thank God the church did not only accommodate me but they summoned the cream of their resources for our marriage counseling within such short notice.

Once again, God helped me pull through difficult circumstances and He continued to roll me along the obstacle course as declared in Proverbs: He guards the paths of justice, and preserves the way of His saints (Prov. 2:8). My faith knew no bounds. Although I was a teacher, I did not inform any of the teaching staff about my impending marriage. The staff welfare association of which I was a member had very rich packages for such events, but I traded that for secrecy. This showed how much of a premium I put on secrecy concerning my marriage. Still, the larger portion of my family members had no idea what I had arranged for myself. By the grace of God, I had largely succeeded in keeping things under wraps up to a few weeks before my wedding. I short-circuited the customary and religious requirements. I had bypassed many people and procedures. I felt there was going to be a huge backlash. However, I had always survived doing things in my own way in spite of criticism. I was ready for even more severe reactions for the way I'd handled my marriage processes. I was prepared to push down whatever and whoever stood in my way and head for the ultimate.

From this time forth, I became very assertive and even more aggressive because I was already fully committed. I felt the duty to see our preparations to their conclusion. A sense of "no turning back" saturated my resolve. It was not just a marriage for me but God's purpose being accomplished as well. As it turned out later, there were some who criticized our discretion but never dared to come out in the open. My marriage event was too honorable to make any criticism meaningful. That was how God shut the mouth of my critics. It always reminds me of Daniel in the lion's den.

There was one more challenge I faced three weeks before the marriage. Custom demanded that I informed the head of my maternal family right from the beginning, even before the knocking stage. Traditionally, he had various roles to play in the process up to the point of marriage, yet I had ignored him entirely. There was a particular role that was indispensable and exclusively limited to him or his assign. During the marriage process, he would have to pledge to Sylvia's family that he, as the head of my family, stood behind the marriage and would do his part to make it work whatever it took. This was a very difficult moment for me because he would definitely feel snubbed. Substituting another relative for him without his consent would amount to an even bigger snub. His reaction may, therefore, be negative and that would cast a very dark shadow upon my marriage. Traditionally, if the head of one's family does not favor his or her marriage, the marriage loses huge credibility. Such a situation may resound negatively with the more significant members of the extended family. I thought about this for a while and went on my knees.

A couple of weeks before my marriage, I gathered courage and went to him to request his presence. I braced for the worst. After I had told him of my preparation so far, he looked at me in shock, shook his head and said, "You're crazy." Then, he asked for other details, making sure every step I had taken was in the right order. When he realized that I had finished almost every prior preparation, he rebuked me in a few words. I took it in good humor, but I was not really perturbed. With God behind me, I feared no man. All I needed was his presence. Nothing else mattered to me, however chastising it was. At last, he promised he would attend the marriage ceremony. When I asked to leave, he remarked, "That was bold! You must have a lot of guts to defy traditions like that. You are a brave man. You didn't do well, but I admire your courage and determination." I then recalled Romans: "And we know that all things work together for good to them that love God, to them who are the called according to his purpose." (Rom. 8:28 KJV)

I knew I got him still wondering about things even as I left. He had never seen anything like that since he was born. I understand he kept talking about me even after the marriage with both intrigue and admiration. Intrigued because he realized that he was not the only one in the dark about my marriage preparations, almost everyone else was as well including my biological father. He was filled with admiration because he saw how every preparation had been rightly put in place and witnessed just how smoothly the whole ceremony went without a single hitch. He wondered how I could undertake such a thorough preparation all alone, but I was not really alone as the Father, the Son, and the Spirit were all with me. That is a very huge and powerful team.

On March 2, 2006, two days prior to the marriage and wedding ceremonies, I set off in my father's Mercedes-Benz sedan around 10:00 in the morning. It was a Thursday. With as little as eight hundred Cedis (about $115) left in my pocket, I trusted God to provide and set out alone on a 200-mile plus journey to Winneba via Cape Coast. I drove cautiously and relaxed. I made a couple of stops on the way to make sure I do not get tense. I needed to take every precaution to preserve myself for the wedding and for Sylvia. At one point, I made a detour to the University of Cape Coast to visit Doris, one of Azay's daughters, who was then a student there. I also took the opportunity to inform an acquaintance in a nearby suburb of the impending wedding.

After about two and a half hours, I set off again toward Winneba. The highway between Winneba and the Cape Coast was then under construction, and it was dusty and slow going at some points. In the middle of the trip, Michael Antobreh, who was to be my Best Man, called me to find out if I had arrived safely. When I said I was still on the way, he quickly hung up after promising to call later when I would not be at the steering controls. I finally arrived in the Dadzies' home at nightfall. That night, I realized a whole lot of activities and frantic preparations were underway.

While I managed to keep my side of the marriage under wraps, Sylvia's end had been blown out. The situation had completely got out of her control. Sylvia was so kind and pleasant a lady that whoever encountered her could not resist her affection. I was, therefore, not surprised that so many people from far and near came to offer help on the occasion of her marriage. Sitsofe, our timekeeper in the Tseinoo Group, had arrived the previous day to help her Tseinoo mate and keep her company. I encountered Sylvia briefly as she had a lot of grooming to do (all for me). I hovered around for a while and went indoors. If I did not know exactly what was going on, I was not worried either.

To avoid complications, I had kept my side of the deal simple. However, what I saw on Sylvia's side was in sharp contrast. I was very lost. I realized it was not something she or I could control any longer. Her parents, aunties, uncles, brothers, cousins, friends, and staff mates all had their hands on deck. Sylvia brought me something to eat. After that we sat down to chat for a few minutes. I wanted to know how far her preparations had gone. It was good to hear she had more hands than she needed for the various activities. I recounted my journey that had begun that morning. I removed my few belongings from the trunk of the car and went to sleep by 10:00 P.M. I was tired from the day-long driving. Michael, my Best Man, called for the second time to find out how I was doing. He assured me he would be coming the following day, the eve of the occasion. On that note, I retired to bed.

The next day was March 3, 2006. I woke up rather early. I was obsessed with what was going to take place the following day, specifically my wedding. I stayed indoors for most of the morning. After I had showered and dressed, Mrs. Dadzie brought me breakfast. I was expecting some key members of my family to arrive later in the day for the occasion. I was also expecting my good friend, Vincent, that evening. While pondering over these issues, I learned that Sylvia needed to rush to the hair dresser's to put finishing touches to her hair before the Bride Decorator arrived. I offered to drop her off as time was not on her side. Traditionally, I was not supposed to see her on the wedding eve until she was presented to me at the marriage ceremony the following day. However, all the stakeholders agreed that I should be allowed to take her, and I did. From the beginning we had broken most of the traditional rules and conventions. This was the eve of our wedding, and we still kept breaking them. God gave us favor in the eyes of the movers and shakers who acquiesced to our uniqueness. I saw the hand of

God in all of these things. He gave us total control over the affair. I quickly took Sylvia in the Benz and dropped her at the hairdresser's I waited for her to finish and rushed her home. She quickly disappeared into her room to continue her grooming. At about 12:30 P.M., Mrs. Dadzie brought me lunch. I could not really savor the meal because my mind started drifting and wandering as the clock ticked toward the marriage. I realized I was becoming tense. I left the house in the Benz and headed for the beach where Sylvia and I had sat the first time I visited her at Winneba. I wanted to cool down my mind and spirit to avoid too much tension.

Until this time, I had been very relaxed and confident. I chose a very quiet place at the beach and sat down to think over how far we had come. I thought of what lay ahead and felt that was the most critical. If anything should go wrong the next day, all of our successes so far would come to naught. We were almost there, yet it felt so far. If there was ever any time that I needed prayers, this was it, and I did not hesitate. I started praying and waiting. Intermittently, I would stop and walk the length of the beach watching the wonders of the waves and feeling the coolness of the breeze.

At times the thought of Sylvia would flash through my head. I was wondering how much of the pressure she could take. I had not been able to get really close to her ever since I arrived. I also did not have any genuine assessment of how her preparation was going so far. I wanted to be by her in order to lend a helping hand to make her load light as I did at school during our studies. I was stimulated to pray for her all the more.

While still admiring nature and praying intermittently, I had a call from Abraham. He had arrived at the Winneba town in his van with his wife and other close family members on board. This was the first batch of my family members. They were not familiar with the town, so I drove to meet them and escorted them to the Dadzie's private home where I stayed. Michael, my Best Man, also walked in unannounced. Soon after, Vincent called, and I went to meet him at yet another part of the town.

I was still chatting with Vincent, when a call came in from a cousin of mine. He had arrived with the second batch of family members in a station wagon, a Landcruiser Prado, which would also serve as the Bride's Carriage come the next day. The occupants included my father, my mother's representative, and other significant family members. I hurried to meet them in the house where Sylvia's parents had already welcomed them. All my family members who had arrived got together in a standing meeting to discuss preparations so far. They asked about the venues for the traditional marriage ceremony and the wedding. I briefed them on my preparations up to that time but could not tell them about Sylvia's preparations in any detail as I had not chatted with her to any appreciable length. I had also not spoken with Mr. and Mrs. Dadzie that much. "From the look of things, I have no doubt everything is on course," I assured them.

From there, we broke the meeting, and everybody went to his or her reserved accommodations to prepare for the next day's activities. I moved indoors with Michael, my Best Man, to try on our costumes for the events. We had arranged to dress in the same clothes. We had our coats and pairs of trousers sown from the same fabric material. We had also bought two sets of dress shirts of the same color and texture. Our ties and cuff links were the same as well, with black shoes to match. If anything was different, it was the shape of our faces for our skin complexion was even similar. We fixed our ties, polished our shoes, ironed our attire, and hung everything for the next day.

There was one thing vital still left to be done. Sylvia and I had to rehearse our vows before the wedding, and it was less than fourteen hours away. We should have done this long ago but for the distance between our respective cities. If customarily I was not supposed to see Sylvia, I would do so one more time, not in the morning or afternoon but very late in the night.

At about 11:00 P.M. that night, I took Sylvia, her Maid of Honor, and my Best Man to the car. Sitsofe could not leave her only female colleague in the Tseinoo Group, so she offered to accompany us. She had stayed mostly by Sylvia's side over the few days leading to the occasion. Together, we drove to the chapel where the wedding was to take place the next day. Michael could not hide his admiration upon seeing the officiating pastor for our wedding still waiting with a smile on his face after all this delay. He had been waiting for more than five hours. Knowing we needed enough rest for the next day's event, he quickly ushered us in and began coaching us through our roles and movements for the ceremony the next day. In a little less than an hour, we were headed back home. We arrived a few minutes past midnight and each of us headed straight to bed, which concluded the day before our marriage.

CHAPTER 19

THE MARRIAGE CEREMONY

*"The king shall joy in Thy strength O Lord; and in Thy salvation
how greatly shall he rejoice! Thou hast given him his heart's
desire, and hast not withholden the request of his lips."*
—Psalm 21:1-2 (KJV)

Indeed, the Lord was about to fulfill the biggest desire I had. Slowly, the day crawled out of the night. The daylight began to peep through the window curtains as if to say, "Hello, where are you? I am here for you." It was the much-awaited day and month of the year 2006. The month and day that would be marked by marriage, merriment, and our wedding. March 4 had finally arrived but stealthily. It did not show any sign of the beauty and pageantry that would later erupt in it. Yet, it was the March that would bring into culmination the fulfillment of a long-kept promise, a well-rewarded patience, an honor rightly bestowed, and a burden of bachelorhood rolled off the shoulders of diligent stewards. It was the month that would bring the peace that transcends the future and a day like no other. The exceptional beauty of the day became apparent as the sun began to rise. The extra brightness of the sun coupled with the

187

copious breeze from the sea told of its significance. Nature was at her artistic and decorative best, no doubt. As the sun slowly rose, the breeze never stopped refreshing us with its cooling winds. It was a dreamy weather as in a fairy tale, something the officiating pastor noted in his remarks. The last batch of my family members had arrived from Kumasi at dawn, including my benefactor cousin, Azay, in whose home I had been living for the previous twelve consecutive years. I was very happy to see him in the company of his lovely wife, Sister Pat. He had also brought along one of his children, Gloria, who was needed in the team of our flower girls. The head of my family also came with the Azay's.

As early as 6:00 A.M., all other family members joined me in Mr. Dadzie's private home where I had been residing for the previous two days. After the usual pleasantries, we drove to Sylvia's extended family house a short distance away to perform the traditional (customary) part of the marriage. The approach was both traditional and Christian, so many issues were commingled. The traditional methods of marriage were followed but they were done in the spirit of the Christian faith. Both Sylvia and I were staunch believers, hence we did not subscribe to anything unworthy or that which conflicted with our faith. Where tradition conflicted with our faith, we requested modification. For instance, all customary practices requiring the use of alcohol or strong drinks were either scrapped, replaced with currency or something more acceptable to our faith.

By 7:00 A.M., my family, including myself, had gathered outside Sylvia's extended family house waiting to be ushered in. Her family members were already seated, and they were ready to receive us. An emissary came to take us in. Led by our spokesman, Uncle Brenya, the same uncle of mine who spoke on my behalf during the knocking ceremony, we filed into the house and greeted Sylvia's family by the shaking of hands as tradition demanded. We then took our seats and were welcomed by the elders of Sylvia's family. Prayer was said to initiate the process—traditionally, this would have been the pouring of libation, but as Christians we started with prayer instead.

The Dadzie family spokesman asked my family about our mission to their house that morning. Uncle Brenya got up and spoke metaphorically in the local language. He indicated that one of his nephews (that was me) had seen a beautiful "flower" in their house that he wanted to pluck, hence our presence in their midst. In traditional ceremonies like this, local languages are strictly used, and proverbs are commonplace. Most messages are crisply transmitted in aphorisms and metaphors to outwit the uninformed.

At this time, we entered into the introduction stage. Sylvia's family members introduced themselves first, followed by mine. Their spokesman asked us what instruments we brought to enable us to "pluck such a beautiful but thorny flower." By implication, he meant the dowry. Uncle Brenya then asked to be brought forward what we had assembled. Mr. Dadzie had been careful not to put too much demand on me in terms of the dowry he proposed. It included a Holy Bible, envelopes of modest amounts of money for the Bride's father, mother, and siblings, a large travel bag containing clothing, ladies' shoes among others, a sewing machine, and crates of soft drinks. Each item was traditionally significant, but I will not go into those details in this book.

My uncle presented the Holy Bible first before the rest of the dowry. Once Sylvia's family had viewed the items, they asked to see specifically who amongst us was the one who wanted to pluck their "flower." That was when I was introduced. I was still shy, but this was the time for courage, so I mustered some. From then on, I was going to be in the spotlight—no time for shyness and hiding now. I was put in the center of the gathering and given a seat. Next, they sent for the bride. She had been hidden all this while in one of the rooms in the interior part of the house.

If there was ever any time when I had to be very vigilant, this was it. More often than not, the bride's family would present a look-alike of the bride to fool the bridegroom just as Laban did to Jacob with Leah, when in fact, he thought he had married Rachel. (Gen. 29:15-30). Fortunately, they kept it simple. Previously, Sylvia and I had discussed wearing clothes made of the same fabric, design, and color. My tailor and her seamstress sewed the same fabric materials for us so, when I saw that the clothes she was wearing matched mine, I knew she was the one even before I could effectively look at her face. They asked me if that was the flower I had come to pluck. I responded in the affirmative, and they sat Sylvia beside me, to my right.

At this point, there was an uproar amidst clapping. I was half conscious and half in dreamland. As tradition demanded, Sylvia had to be briefed about what had taken place prior to her arrival. Her permission was also needed on whether or not the family should accept the gift of the dowry items on her behalf. Lastly, Sylvia needed to reaffirm in the presence of the gathering whether she, indeed, accepted my proposal. This duty was delegated to her pastor, Mr. Alexander Yawson, who would also officiate the wedding ceremony. As soon as he got up, he made an observation. Consciously or unconsciously, Sylvia had slipped her left hand over her chair's armrest and rested it on my right lap. Upon seeing that, the pastor remarked that he needed to ask her whether she agreed to my proposal. However, looking at where her hand was resting at that moment, it was a forgone conclusion. There erupted another uproar and laughter amidst shouting. When the noise died down, he took the engagement ring, raised it up, and blessed it. He led me as I slipped it onto Sylvia's finger followed by a thunderous applause. Before the man of God took his seat, he held our hands and prayed with us. The spokesmen on both sides asked us to retake our seats. Between the two of them, there was a lot of humor, which kept both the families and the gathered well-wishers laughing most of the time. The spokesman for Sylvia's family took the stage again and asked which people were specifically behind my marriage.

Traditionally, there ought to be particular people who volunteer to guide, mentor, and be responsible for newlyweds to ensure the marriage survives until husband and wife gain a footing in the marriage arena. To this, my uncle spokesman got up and introduced the head of my family, my father, and my mother's step-sister, who was a proxy for my deceased mother, as the main mortal pillars from my side. The mentors from Sylvia's side included her Uncle John, her father, and her mother. Uncle Brenya gave our address in Kumasi, specifically the suburb and the residential address.

While this was going on, Sylvia's family were distributing souvenirs to all who had come to witness the marriage ceremony, especially my family members. Unfortunately, the crowd was greater than expected so some guests did not get any. That was something Sylvia felt very uneasy about. Even to this day she regrets some went away from her marriage without a souvenir. We planned something modest, but people's reactions got out of hand. There was a familiarization on the floor before the closing prayer, and by 9:30 A.M., the closing prayer had been said. Sylvia got up from my side and went to get ready for the wedding ceremony, which was to take place in about two hours' time in the chapel. We were served breakfast at the same venue. I ate with the few male members from my family who had attended the ceremony. That was the first time I'd had the chance to talk to Azay since I left his home three days prior. He was at his usual humorous best. He kept us laughing at the table all the time.

THE WEDDING

After breakfast, Michael and I left Sylvia's family's house and drove to her parent's private home where my room was. We started preparing for the wedding ceremony, which was less than two hours away. We dressed in our matching clothes and accessories and headed for the chapel. By midday we were in the chapel. It was surprisingly very breezy that day. A lot of people were already seated at the chapel by the time we arrived, and I could still see many people trooping in. We were directed to take our reserved seats. My seat and Sylvia's were in the very front of the middle pew. Michael sat behind me with an empty seat to his right meant for the maid of honor. Behind them were three seats reserved for our flower girls.

Michael's command of his duties began to show as we waited for the arrival of the bride. Every now and then he would get up from his seat and wipe my face and neck to keep me sweat- and dust-free for my precious bride. He had been a Groom's Man prior so he was very proficient and professional. Intermittently, he would chip a word into my ears that made me laugh and smile. He really kept tension from getting the better of me. I could not tell how long we waited but I saw the chapel gradually filling to capacity even before the bride arrived.

Once I began hearing the slang word *Dondoo* (a slogan for newlyweds), I knew Sylvia was near. I looked back but she was nowhere to be found. As we continued to wait, the noise became more frequent, a sign that she was getting closer. I did not want to be looking back every now and then, lest people would interpret it as impatience. I rather guessed Sylvia's approach and nearness by the loudness of the noise behind me.

When the noise of the gathered crowd became continuously deafening, I knew Sylvia had arrived at the chapel. Then I heard the entry hymn, "Count Your Blessings" begin. I was right; the hymn had confirmed her arrival. Sylvia and I had been careful to select very resounding hymns for the occasion. "Happy Day", "'Tis So Sweet to Trust in Jesus," and "To God Be the Glory" were the other hymns we'd selected. Slowly, putting one foot after another, the bride's party marched forward. I stayed stiff and forward looking until I saw a man's black shoe and a lady's silver shoe step up from behind in the aisle to my right. A daughter's hand in her father's, they turned toward where I was seated. Gently and delicately, Mr. Dadzie lowered Sylvia into her seat beside me to the right. I observed all that through the right corner of my eyes. Sylvia was veiled yet I could not resist stealing glances at her from the right corner of my eyes. She had beautifully petalled flowers in the colors of white, blue, and silver to match her wedding colors in her left hand. Her hair was very dark and shiny. Smoothed from the edges, it looked as silky as black satin threads. It was pulled up at the top of her head and designed to a near twisting strand at the back of her head. The lines in her neck made terrace-like rings to add to her charm. Her arms were half gloved by lace that went up to her elbow. However, from her elbow to her shoulder showed bare flesh and radiant, smooth skin. Her beautiful contours showed elegantly in her long-tailed gown with her cheeks ever shining from within the veil like a beam from under water. Her silvery feet, half-hidden by her white gown, looked like that of Cinderella. For the first time, I felt I was seeing an angel sit by my side on earth.

Meanwhile, Michael kept fanning me from behind. I turned and told him that I was not sweating. "Hold tight, bro., you soon will," he replied. I nearly burst out loud in laughter, but I resisted as the function had already entered its formal phase. I struggled to keep myself from bursting out loud given the humorous nature of his remark. To help me in that course, I decided not to look at Michael's face again. I was afraid the next word from his mouth may break my resistance to laughter. I refocused on my bride. Sylvia was all smiles when the officiating minister took the podium to formally announce the occasion. She knew her moment of glory had arrived.

The chapel resounded with a joyful noise after the announcement. We were invited to the podium to begin the process of the exchange of vows. Together we climbed up the podium respectively escorted by our Best Man and Maid of Honor. We stood facing each other with the officiating minister in the middle. He was to my right and to Sylvia's left, but he was centered between us. The man of God spoke in English as he announced that our marriage had been duly contracted and that all official actions and documentations had been completed. Therefore, if anybody in the gathering had any reason why we should not be joined together as husband and wife, let that fellow speak then, or forever keep quiet. There was a pause for a moment, and the room went silent. Then he resumed his duties.

I was not comfortable being put in the limelight for that long. As soon as I got to the podium, I wished it was over, but it was going to be a long ceremony with vivid elaborations. My mind kept drifting from the podium to the background noise and back to the podium. Everything unfolded like a dream. I felt like a butterfly floating in an unknown space. I just felt like I was following proceedings while Sylvia was very spirited and full of smiles throughout. I remember the pastor calling for the one who was giving up Sylvia for marriage to come forward. Mr. Dadzie stepped forward, held his daughter's hand, and declared he was the one. The pastor asked him to confirm his statement, which he did without hesitation. Mr. Dadzie held Sylvia's wrist and extended her hand into mine. Immediately, a sharp contrast flashed back into my mind. Here is a man who once refused to allow his daughter to come with me even on a visit. But this day, he is readily and smilingly offering the hand of the same daughter to me. I knew my faith had worked. I felt a sense of gratitude to God, a deep respect for Mr. Dadzie, and a sense of accomplishment on my part.

Once I took hold of his daughter's hand, Mr. Dadzie let go of Sylvia's hand to signify the transfer of responsibility. We remained that way, holding hands throughout the exchange of vows. The pastor led me to say my vows first. At the conclusion, "till death do us part," the chapel came alive with a noise of approval amidst shouts of *Amutu-u-u-u-u-u-u! Amutu-u-u-u-u-u! Amutu* was a slogan initiated by Michael when we were students of the University of Ghana. It became very popular among a group of students who studied with us at a specific spot behind the Physics Department building. The place was shady and airy in the day and very cool at night. So, we preferred that place to the lecture halls, even to the library. Sylvia's turn to exchange vows came. With a soothing voice, a distinctively articulate tone, and in a rhythmic pattern, Sylvia recited every sentence after the pastor with the utmost clarity and charm. The crowd was wowed, and before Sylvia could finish her last sentence, the chapel erupted into wild applause and shouts of "You deserve it!" Then, came the moment everybody was waiting for—the lifting of the veil.

At this point, the pastor stepped back and asked me to go ahead. There were shouts and noises of all kinds from all corners of the chapel hall. Michael came from behind me and wiped my hands. Slowly, I proceeded, folding the veil into my hand and gradually rolling it upwards. Sylvia was looking at me with a broad smile all the while. As I got to her chin, I did some little theatrics. I stopped, looked closer through the net and let go the entire veil. The noise from the background became intense. Michael came forward and recleaned my hands for another shot at the enterprise. I turned toward Sylvia again and restarted.

Slowly and gradually, I pulled her veil well up, revealing Sylvia's full, smiling face. I flipped it to the back of her head, gave her a quick peck on the left cheek, and embraced her. I hugged her lightly, but she grabbed me tighter and rubbed my back with her right palm while holding her flowers in the left hand. It could not have felt better. There was a good amount of sensation in there. In most weddings, the bridegroom would kiss the bride at this stage, but I had previously discussed with Sylvia that I would not feel comfortable kissing her in public. I told her that I was known for decency and decorum. I would not want to sacrifice that reputation for the sake of the wedding. Sylvia replied that she knew another reason why I did not want to kiss her on the podium. She got me curious, so I asked her what that reason was. "The main reason is because you are shy, but I understand," she said. Well, she was right and knew me more than I credited her for. With that, we agreed on a compromise—a peck—which I found not too invasive. By this time, the noise in the chapel had become uncontrollable. I overhead a man bursting through the noise with a dominating male voice in the following words, "Since 1996," in reference to the first time Sylvia and I became friends on campus. I recognized the voice to be that of Eli Moto, an extroverted colleague of ours at Mount Mary College.

When the noise had subsided a little bit, the pastor asked us to turn to the congregation. Before she could turn, Sylvia needed assistance from her Maid of Honor with the tail of her gown. I had already turned and was facing the crowd before Sylvia did. The noise began to rise again. I felt Sylvia quickly and forcefully slip her right hand into mine as if to say, "Don't forget we're married now." I grabbed her hand quickly as the pastor pronounced us husband and wife. The noise regained its crescendo. When it ebbed, the pastor asked to pray for us. The flower girls quickly brought pillows for us to kneel on. The pastor prayed for us after which we went down to take our seats. We were directed to change our seating order. Sylvia sat on my left instead of my right as before. I was oblivious, but Michael made sure of everything. Hymns and songs were sung before the next scheduled event of the program.

It was time for the sermon. The word of admonition for the occasion was given by one Evangelist Martin Boateng. By design, he was the same person who had previously preached at Sylvia's parents' marriage blessing some years earlier. This is when I woke up from what was seemingly akin to proceedings in a fairy tale. Before he would even utter a word of admonition, he told the congregation that he was going to ask me to do something that would serve as an introduction to his message. He would not say immediately what he wanted me to do. What shook me most was when he intimated, "I know he is a man." Immediately, my mind went into an uncontrollable spin. I am sure it made a hundred thousand revolutions per minute.

What at all does this man want me to do to show my manhood? I wondered. It even seemed creepy. I started feeling hot and could feel my sweat. My heart rate went up. Then I remembered Michael's words earlier on. Truly, the sweat period had arrived. Finally, the Evangelist said, "I want Aaron to lift Sylvia up." Phew! That got me really sweating. I was very much relieved. *Sylvia would not be too heavy,* I said to myself. I looked back at Michael who shot up from his seat like a bullet and stood by my side. Sylvia's Maid of Honor was also at hand to ready her for the lift. When all was set, I grabbed Sylvia's back with my left arm and lifted her feet off the ground with my right. In this way, she fell into my bosom. I spun her round and set her down gently. To this date I cannot imagine how the idea of spinning Sylvia around came to mind but going this extra mile added even more beauty to the exercise.

We retook our seats and Evangelist Martin Boateng could not be more grateful and happier. He was boisterous and beamed with a lot of energy. He preached so forcefully that he was literally drenched in sweat by the time he ended his sermon. His message bordered on divorce in the church. It was one of the most relevant messages for the occasion. Backed by statistics, he touched on how children of God lose steam so easily after marriage. He emphasized the need to still be willing and happy to "lift our spouses years after marriage." He dubbed it the "Maintenance Culture of Marriage." More hymns and choruses followed as we prepared to go for the signatures. With the song "Happy Day," the officiating minister, Pastor Yawson, led us slowly to the Mission House for the signatures.

I tucked Sylvia's right arm loosely unto my left side as we took measured steps down the aisle. During this period, my eyes met those of a prominent person whose presence ignited a sense of honor in me. He was Professor William Baah-Boateng of the Economics Department, the University of Ghana. This man and I have been childhood friends from our elementary school days. I nodded at him to signal acknowledgment, and he responded with a wave of his hands. When we stepped out of the chapel, I was humbled to see the overflow of people outside the chapel who had come to witness the occasion. They could not get a seat inside the chapel. After the signatures, we returned to the chapel for the presentation of the Marriage Certificate. Sylvia received it on our behalf from Mr. Ahima, a marriage committee representative from Ash-Town Baptist Church, my church. After the benediction, we went for the pictures. With Sylvia's hand still tucked into my side, we walked slowly down the aisle and out to the side of the chapel.

A lot of people were already gathered outside when we took our stand as groups were called. They gathered around us while we took several pictures. After the wedding, Michael, Ekua-Atta, (the Maid of Honor), Sylvia, and I got into the Bridal Carriage and drove off to the beach for some memorable fun. Sylvia and I played the "Catch Me If You Can" game at the beach for the cameras. She broke away from me and ran in the sand with her silver shoes still on while I pursued her till I caught up. I lifted her again at the beach, and we posed in different ways for the camera.

From the beach, we got back into the Bridal Carriage and went to the Assembly Hall of the University College of Winneba where a reception was planned for the guests and dignitaries. Everyone was already seated. The flower girls had also arrived in another vehicle and were outside waiting when we arrived. We quickly filed into procession and made a royal entry. Amidst shouts of *Amutu,* we made for the high table and took our seats. A prayer was said and the dignitaries were invited to join us at the high table. Uncle John took chairmanship of the event. This was the very reason that prompted him to ask us for the postponement of the wedding date. He took the microphone and did not hesitate to blurt out his gratitude for our patience with him. He gave a short address as chairman's response and took his seat. Two singing groups had been invited to entertain the guests. While they entertained us with choice local songs, the guests were served refreshments amidst dancing and merrymaking. At a point in time, the festivities paused for the cutting of the wedding cake. We were led by Mrs. Veronica Nyarko, the then Principal of the Holy Child High School. After a short address, she led us to cut the cake. Astonishingly, she turned the language into French in the concluding part of her address, something I never knew she was capable of. I am sure the majority of the guests did not understand, but her remarks were intended for us and both of us understood. We took our seats and continued the refreshments. All of a sudden, Michael got up and took the microphone. He gave the Best Man's toast proposal but before I could respond, Sylvia asked to sing. That gave me time to think as I sat beside her. With her sweet voice, she sang to the glory of God. I could not resist joining her in the concluding part of the song. I then took the microphone to respond to the toast proposal. I touched on my vow of celibacy and the fact that I had laid down some measures according to my faith. I trusted God to lead and reward me and what they were seeing was the exact result of my relationship with God. I admonished the guests to also challenge God and themselves in a similar fashion and assured them that He would never disappoint them.

Another period of singing and dancing followed. We were invited to come down to the floor and dance for the guests. It was quite a challenge, because I was not particularly good at dancing. I held Sylvia's gown and gradually, we descended the stairs onto the dancing floor amidst songs of gospel praise from the disc jockey's table. I did not know where I got my dancing skills from. I realized I was dancing well as the crowd gradually joined us on the floor. Sandwiched between the guests, Sylvia and I danced to relieve our feet. My *Amutu* colleagues from the University of Ghana came closer to me, and we danced together. Unknown to me, they had hatched a plan to lift me up unawares. I saw one of them interacting with Michael. Afterwards, Michael whispered into Sylvia's ears, but I was not bothered. I was too busy dancing. Little did I know they were seeking her permission for what they wanted to do with me. While still dancing, I felt myself being lifted high all of a sudden from behind. Two of my friends had lifted me onto their shoulders as I waved in the air through the dance. It was such a lovely surprise. To this day, I remember that moment with a lot of pride, fun, and nostalgia. Afterwards, they dropped me for another bout of dancing until Sylvia and I headed back to the high table.

By this time, the day had been spent, but some of the guests remained with us still. Uncle John gave his closing remarks after which a vote of thanks was given and the closing prayer was said to mark the end of the function. As convention demanded, we came down and stood on the floor while the guests individually took turns to shake our hands in a congratulatory manner. As the guests were many, that consumed a considerable amount of time. That was also when we got time to briefly encounter friends and loved ones who had not gotten the chance to speak to us throughout the wedding. Sylvia and I went out to the prairie to take even more pictures after which we went home in the Bridal Carriage. It was almost 8:00 P.M. when we arrived.

On arrival, I saw most of my family members gathered in Mr. and Mrs. Dadzies' home. Sylvia and I stopped at the entrance where they were gathered taking stock of the day's activities. We sat down in their midst and joined the discussion for a while. We were very tired that evening. They asked us to go to bed early and get to know ourselves better as the following day was going to be another busy day for us. It was going to be a Thanksgiving Sunday in the church to climax our marriage. At about 8:30 P.M. we begged leave of them, went in to change and left to take up our reservation in a nearby hotel. Surprisingly, neither of us was in a hurry. It was enough that we had ended the drought. We sat on the plush bed beside each other. It was time for us to recount our stories. We had come a long way together, and we both wanted to recount the memories of our lives.

For the first time, I revealed the specifics of my covenant with God to a human being. I narrated in detail how far I had come up to this point. The trials and temptations I had endured while powered by God's grace, the challenges I had gone through keeping this secret to myself, the difficulty of the marriage preparation, all the sacrifices I had to make in order to get to this point, the walls of tradition that I had to break through, my fears, my hopes, and more. Sylvia listened with rapt attention, much interest, and absorption. She seemed to be awed by the amount of secrecy that had clouded my life's agenda all this while.

Even more surprising to her was the fact that I kept my covenant with God secret from her during all those years of our friendship, a decade to be precise. She trusted me all right and considered me a very simple person. She had no idea how loaded and complex my life's goal was, as I showed no outward signs of such nature. I always kept a calm composure even when overwhelmed. When I told Sylvia how she had unknowingly fulfilled each sign pertaining to the covenant, she could not believe her ears. I asked her if she remembered the last day of our teaching practice (internship). She remembered the occasion and the place very well. Then I quizzed her again, "Do you remember asking me if I would like to live my life with you when we sat on the veranda?" Sylvia did not remember ever asking the Golden Question. She reacted, "I do not see even how I would throw such a question to a man in our culture. Yes, after knowing you I wanted you to be my man but I would not be that crazy to throw it at you so overtly. Moreover, the odds were too much against any relationship beyond just being friends." She paused briefly and resumed, "You were so hostile to relationships that I even had to think twice whenever I wanted to smile at you. I remember you proposed the Tuesday after our teaching practice when we met in the classroom. I never knew your proposal was prompted by a question I had earlier asked," she emphasized. I was not surprised either. In response, I gave an elaborate speech: "That is another reason why I believe God was behind it. We were about to part ways, and God knew I needed it for my next step. I needed some revelations to show that you were the very person God had chosen to be my future wife, and God made sure I had that difficult proof before we parted. Initially, we were randomly selected and paired together for the teaching practice but God had planned it. Even subsequent allegations from worried observers could not meaningfully separate us. We were separated in different ways, but we still ended up in the same school. Nothing could thwart God's plan for us. "I believe the Spirit of God prompted you to give me a cue. Otherwise, I could have forgotten about you when life's waves battered my memories," I concluded. She looked at me quizzically, still with a lot of surprise on her face. I reaffirmed, "Yes, you did. God knew I needed it to make a vital decision, so He caused you to speak in fulfillment of the most difficult term of the covenant. I am not surprised that you are not aware of what came out of your own mouth. It was for me. I was aware of my vows so I noted it carefully when you uttered it. It might have been a random utterance for you but for me it was crucial," I declared.

There was a quiet and solemn moment afterwards. Sylvia was apparently astonished but grateful at the same time for the revelation. She heaved a great sigh and gazed at the ceiling. Then, she said in a low voice, almost in a whisper, "Glory be to God." She had tried to recall the past, but every conversation she remembered about that day could not have led her to such an outburst. After that solemn reflection, as if she was playing back old memories, Sylvia looked at me and intoned, "I now understand why you behaved the way you did when I first saw you at college. I felt you were pretending or hiding something, which made me initially curious and suspicious about you. This notwithstanding, everything else about you was good, even excellent." For the second time she uttered the words, "Thank You, Jesus".

Something had struck Sylvia's mind that I did not know. She wondered at how her life's objectives mostly coincided with those of mine. How our paths could have led from the forest zone on my part and the coast on her part, to cross on the eastern plains initially, and finally merge and melt together at the coast was a mystery to her. My spirit perfectly agreed. It set both of us wondering as she regained composure. Sylvia told me that she had also set equally high moral and godly standards for herself. Even though she did not enter into any covenant, her determination to stick to those standards was equally uncompromising and resilient. She would not sacrifice sexual purity and godliness for anything else in the world. The congruence of our resolutions had not happened in a vacuum. "It is purely an act of God," as Sylvia put it. We never knew each other, and we were quite distant from each other. For two people from diverse backgrounds in different geographical areas to have such an alignment of life's objectives and principles was quite baffling to her. Sylvia could not be more grateful to God who made all that happen. She looked at me and said in a very thankful manner, "I'm an answer to your prayer and you are a reward for my godly tenacity." I could not agree with her more then and now. She continued to tell me how her life had unfolded over the years. She revealed to me that many men expressed interest in her, but she had no love for them such as would lead to marriage. In spite of their wealth and lofty promises, she found no reason to accept their proposals.

In contrast, I had no wealth or riches, but Sylvia felt very comfortable with me and would readily accept my proposal if it came. In retrospect, she reckoned, it was all divinely inspired. "God put the love for you in my heart beyond measure. We were really made for each other," she deduced. I nodded in agreement with a bashful smile. Sylvia emphasized that it had been a challenge for her along the way. At a point in time during her studies at the university, she was convinced I was the one she wanted to marry. However, she had anxious moments when she could not pinpoint whether I had the same affection for her. My reluctance to discuss marriage, let alone come forward in plain terms kept her in great suspense and tension.

I never knew I'd given her all those hard times and felt very sorry. However, I did not express that verbally to her. I was too cheerful to express a sorry state.

Both of us believed staunchly in God, we had similar life principles, we had the same uncompromising resolutions for our lives, we had similar objectives for life that coincided in a shared destiny, and we had triumphed as individuals in very challenging times. Now here we were to carry out the rest of our journey hand-in-hand. Our marriage was a harbinger of things to come: unanimity, oneness of mind, body, soul, and spirit, the desire to worship God, love and share each other. We had so many things in common. Against such there would be no effective weapon. If we'd succeeded individually, we were bound to repeat our success on an even greater scale as a couple. We believed that if we continued that path going forward, we would be the object of God's everlasting blessing. We could not figure it out, but we felt we would be blessed without measure.

On that agreement, Sylvia got up, pulled my nose as she would have done in college, and headed for the bathroom. I was very grateful a woman of her caliber loved me and had given me her heart. I did not consider myself handsome, I was not rich, I was not earthly royalty, but a woman fit for a king gave me her heart and body. Thus, I ended my sexless life thirteen days before my thirty-fifth birthday. That also ended her twenty-eight and a half years of pure celibate life. I felt very lucky, rewarded, and loved. I had never felt such an air of relief. All my anxiety about the burdens of marriage, the difficulty of choosing the right person, and the ability to love a woman were lifted off my shoulders that day. It was a relief beyond description. Prior, these anxieties used to be matters of concern for me. Sylvia had played a significant role in propelling me to this level of achievement. No wonder she has been a major influence in our fight to keep the faith. I had never been happier until I married my beloved wife, and ever since I have had no regrets and even wish I could marry her again and again.

Sylvia and I stepping out of the chapel.

Sylvia and I at the beach.

CHAPTER 20

THE ICING ON THE CAKE

"Whenever we follow God's principles, we receive God's provisions and enjoy His promise."
—Dr. Myles Munroe

The next day, March 5, 2006, was the icing on the cake. We got up early in the morning and came back to the Dadzies' private home. There, the groomers had arrived an hour earlier waiting for Sylvia. She went straight into grooming while I got prepared with Michael. We finished hours before Sylvia and her bridal trail would. We were expected at the chapel at 9:00 A.M. but we got there two hours later. The entire congregation was waiting for us. I was both sorry and humbled when I realized the service had paused awaiting our arrival.

As soon as we went in, the officiating minister who had conducted our wedding started the proceedings. The service went very well, and the topic of the reading focused on "The One God Blesses." In the course of his sermon, the minister observed how the previous day, being our wedding day, had been very different. The breeze that refreshed the day was unusual. It was unusual to have a crowd that

207

large when there were as many as four different funeral ceremonies going on simultaneously. To have your wedding unknowingly on the very birthday of the officiating minister was also unusual. To the minister, it was a single ceremony but a double occasion. All of these signs pointed to the fact that God had blessed us as a couple along with anyone who lent a hand or partook in it. "We all share in God's blessing," he concluded. Sylvia and I were invited to the front to face the congregation during which I was asked how it felt to have married. I did not hesitate to point out the uncertainty that lay ahead while being grateful for what had been accomplished so far. With Sylvia standing by my side, I compared the situation to a morsel of food in the mouth. I told the congregation that we had just bitten the marriage food and were yet to chew, let alone swallow it. Therefore, not much could be said about the taste. The congregation broke into laughter. Then I continued, "However, if proceedings so far are anything to go by, then being married promises to be fantastic." After that short opinion, we were asked to take our seats. The rest of the church service continued. Upon closing, we filed out in the same fashion as the previous day after the wedding ceremony to take even more pictures.

THE BUFFET

After the church service, we went home quickly to prepare for a buffet set in our honor. We had initially envisaged a small wedding ceremony, but then it got out of hand. We had planned a humble lunch, but Uncle John had elevated it to a buffet. I never dreamed of going to a buffet with Sylvia, let alone of having one organized in our honor. That told us how the Lord blessed and honored us. We quickly changed into our dinner dresses. Sylvia still had her stuff in her room, so she went to dress there.

When she stepped out, I nearly somersaulted. She was more than gorgeous and irresistibly attractive. No princess could match up to her stunning beauty. She wore a sea-blue dress held by tiny transparent strings over the shoulders. It was tight on the bust revealing her arms and amazing curves. It spread down to her feet, which were also clad in shoes of a similar color. Her upper back was largely covered by her black, silky hair. I had dressed in my best outfit, yet I was looking at her all the time.

Unaware of my admiration, Sylvia stepped into the outer court where many people were waiting. She walked straight up to me. I took her hand and led her to the car. I opened the door while she sat majestically. I shut the door gently and went around to take the steering wheel. Carefully, we drove to the buffet, which had been set in an outer court of her extended family house. Everything was set up on our arrival, and I was shocked to see dignitaries and other high-ranking people show up. I felt very honored and gave God the glory. There was an uproar when we arrived. People were shouting, clapping, and singing. I took Sylvia's hand as we walked to take our seats among the dignitaries. I could see that all eyes were on Sylvia. Perhaps she had never appeared in such a stupefying beauty to them before. I could not take my eyes off her either. I knew she was beautiful, but I had not seen her in such extraordinary beauty before.

As usual, the function began with prayers after which Uncle John made a brief remark. We went in turns for our food. We were honored to be the first to taste the variety of foods, followed by the dignitaries, then everybody else. Invited group singers entertained us in the background. When the DJ took over the entertainment, we were given the dance floor to display our dancing skills. I felt uncomfortable, but I needed to mask it and do whatever it took to kick up some dancing skills. Sylvia, on the other hand, was on cloud nine. She quickly let go of my hand and began to boogie. She displayed some wonderful skills to the extent that the guests could not wait any longer. They all got to the floor and surrounded us. We were virtually sandwiched by them. After a while, we slipped out back to the table, but the guests continued their merrymaking. My family members had to leave in the middle of the function, because they had more than two hundred and fifty kilometers to cover to get back home. I was very grateful when I heard Mrs. Dadzie had packaged lots of meals for them to enjoy while on the way. The day drew to a close, and after a prayer, the crowd was dismissed. However, the majority of them stayed over to socialize and share goodwill messages with us. When most of the guests and well-wishers had departed, Sylvia, Michael and I went back to the Benz and drove to her parents' private home. After dropping Sylvia off, I took Michael, obviously an outstanding Best Man, to the bus station to catch a bus to Accra where he was based. Sylvia and I spent the night in her parent's home, intending to drive back to Kumasi the following day.

That is how golden snippets of childhood training, juvenile destiny, adolescent struggle, divine intervention, versatility of principle, godly resilience, strength of character, the promise of hope, and the reward of faith were woven together, culminating in a reality fit for a fairy tale. Thanks to the Father who has specific plans for all His obedient children. I have never been happier to date—not because I have no worries or pains; I probably struggle more than the majority of my readers. However, I struggle with delight because of the hope I have in Christ Jesus that my toil will never be in vain.—"Therefore, my beloved brethren, be steadfast, immovable, always abounding in the work of the Lord, knowing that your labor is not in vain in the Lord (1 Cor. 15:58 NASB). It really never has and never will be.

My final word to you, however, is in Hebrews:

> "Let us hold tightly without wavering to the hope we
> affirm, for God can be trusted to keep his promise"
> (Hebrews 10:23 NLT).

To God Be the Glory!

MR & MRS APPIAH-KUBI.

CHAPTER 21

OPEN ADMONITIONS

My son, give attention to my words; incline your ear to my sayings
—Proverbs 4:20 (NASB)

Many are the lessons Sylvia and I have learned and continue to learn about life. A retrospective view of our lives has led to many observations, revelations, and conclusions. These are outlined vividly in another book of ours, *The Lies That Satan Told You,* which is still in the works. However, I would like to share with you some relevant excerpts from that book. The hand of God in our lives—both as individuals and as a couple—is very evident. Even during periods when we did not know He was with us, He still carried out His plans for us and in us. An indispensable ingredient for our success was the deliberate pursuit of godliness, longing and searching for the will of God in our lives. You may have been inspired, and I pray that you do get inspired, to pursue that course. What you should know, however, is that you have to position yourself appropriately to enable God to carry you through. The Apostle Paul admonishes:

"Let not sin therefore reign in your mortal body, that
ye should obey it in the lusts thereof. Neither yield
ye your members as instruments of unrighteousness
unto sin: but yield yourselves unto God, as those that
are alive from the dead, and your members as instruments of righteousness unto God. For sin shall not
have dominion over you: for ye are not under the law,
but under grace." (Rom. 6:12–14 KJV)

Note the words "Let not" at the beginning. It is an instruction that
presumes that you are capable of whatever follows next. You have
been given whatever it takes to accomplish it. You are in control.
What Paul is saying here is that the initiative lies within our individual selves. We have to make a conscious, deliberate, determined,
and firm decision for righteousness. It is not a wish but a willful
decision. All our being—mind, body, spirit, soul—must be primed
for the goal of righteousness, which can only be imputed to us by
Christ. When we have done our part this way, says verse 14, then we
can count on the grace of God to carry us through to the end. Until
we get there, however, the responsibility remains ours and the grace
is God's. There is responsibility even in the grace. For instance, if I
gave you this book as a gift. Though it is free, the gift will not mate-
rialize if you are not willing to stretch forth your hand to receive it.
It is your responsibility to receive and make it work for you. At no
point should we relinquish our responsibility (receiving the grace)
in this course. The grace is, therefore, a special provision from God
and it is freely given to complement our weak ineffectual estate. It
is not a substitute for our will. We have to be willing and prepared
for the grace. With the prevailing sexually promiscuous and perverse
atmosphere, it looks daunting, even impossible, to achieve a sexually straight life. Do not panic but focus on God, the source of your
strength, and He will grant you peace.

"You keep him in perfect peace whose mind is stayed on you, because he trusts in you" (Isa. 26:3 ESV); "And the peace of God, which surpasses all understanding, will guard your hearts and your minds in Christ Jesus" (Phil. 4:7 ESV)

In order to please God, we have to align ourselves to Him. "So then, those who are in the flesh cannot please God" (Rom. 8:8 NKJV). We have to identify with Him without forgetting that God is Spirit. This is where you begin and the following is how God complements: "But if the Spirit of Him who raised Jesus from the dead dwells in you, He who raised Christ from the dead will also give life to your mortal bodies through His Spirit who dwells in you" (Rom. 8□:11 NKJV)

You are partnering with God in the whole enterprise. It is primarily His business, and you are His partner. It is not the other way round. If you regard yourself as the primary person in this partnership, it will be an unsurmountable task. You cannot get anywhere with your strength alone. It is God's business first before it is yours. Your role is to yield to Him, and He will accomplish the rest through grace. Accordingly, we must subject the desires of our body and soul to the direction of His Spirit. Let His will for your life be your guide, and you will realize the providence of God in your life as you take a stand for your spiritual well-being.

THE ABSTINENCE MYTH

> *Sex is a physical sign of a spiritual act.*—Dr. Myles Munroe

In some cultures, many people have bought into the belief that not having sex may lead to antisocial behaviors, thus encouraging people into illicit sex. I want to state categorically that this is not true. It is a misconception orchestrated by the devil, fueled by sinful desires to keep you from observing sexual purity. Purity is the building block of holiness; hence it has huge spiritual benefits. I can attest to this.

Sexual purity keeps us from spiritually staining ourselves with the dirt of sin, the type of which allows the devil to plug directly into our souls and ride us like horses. Impurity punches spiritual holes in our lives, and the enemy takes advantage of them and keep us in his labor camp. Spiritually speaking, it is very difficult for demonic spirits to contend with children of God who are sexually pure. Deliverance ministers testify that anytime you engage in sex; you leave a piece of yourself in the other person and vice versa. This is called a blood covenant. If you have multiple sexual partners, keeping any single relationship successfully will not come easy. You have pieces of many people in you and these pieces compete. This is an unseen spiritual process, hence it is easy to lose sight of it. It is never an achievement to be sleeping with many different people.

Have you wondered why sexually promiscuous bachelors usually become unfaithful spouses? The devil feeds on that weakness of promiscuity. To that end, he devises a myth to catch us young. Tying sexual purity to an unpleasant phenomenon is, therefore, nothing more than the devil's effort to tap into our fleshly desires and cause us to disobey God's Word. And when we disobey God's Word, we fall under a curse. (Deut. 28:15) Sexual purity has never affected my life negatively. On the contrary, observing sexual purity has contributed immensely to the extraordinary success of my marriage. I have never missed my bachelorhood days. To suggest there are perils of abstinence is absolutely false. It saved me from paying child support and allimonies. God needs you to stay sexually pure unto marriage and remain ever faithful to your spouse after marriage.

OBSERVING CHASTITY

> *Let not then your good be evil spoken of: for*
> *the kingdom of God is not meat and drink; but*

righteousness, and peace and joy in the Holy Ghost.—Romans 14:16-17 (KJV)

My wife and I did not have a normal courtship as many would-be couples do. There was virtually no courtship in the modern sense of the word. We stayed away from each other physically. When I started performing the marriage rites, my wife to be had traveled abroad. Many are the would-be couples who could not pass the test of sexual purity due to courtship. My wife and I simply would not make that mistake.

In the early 1990s, one of my few lady acquaintances asked me what my idea about courtship was. I responded point-blank that courtship in the sense of the way many couples do it contemporarily is a trap. The male-female relationship is so magnetic and our culture is becoming so permissive, that courtship has become a recipe for pre-marital sex. It takes no effort at all for courtship to degenerate into fornication. Almost every courtship I knew of or heard about ended in pre-marital sex, which is an abomination. Whether the lovebirds succeed in marrying or not does not change the fact. Sex before marriage regardless of the stage of advancement, even on the night before marriage, is sin. Until the marriage vows have been exchanged and the rites have been performed, you are not married; hence you have no license for sex whether customarily or divinely. Therefore, as young Christians it was dangerous for us to even think about courtship when we had not even obtained our basic certificates of education. In fact, I firmly believed that we had to rely on God to lead us to the right person or forget about marriage completely. I saw the biblical story of Isaac and Rebecca as an example. There was no courtship. I simply believed that if God led Abraham's servant directly to Rebecca when Abraham wanted a wife for his son, it should not be difficult for the same God to do so for all of those who faithfully serve Him. Playing with courtship at that young age would inevitably lead one into sexual sin. "Promise me, O women of Jerusalem, by the gazelles and wild deer, not to awaken love until the time is right"(Song 3:5 NLT). Consequently, one has to be more mature, knowledgeable and sober before considering any path to marriage. That was the last time I heard from that girl. She never wrote back to me even though I did follow up with another friendly letter. I assumed she did not like my response. I was not going to compromise either. It calls for conscious effort toward abstinence to succeed in a clean courtship. This includes physically staying away from each other most of the time and staying outdoors whenever the lovebirds come together. If not, the devil will always prey on your emotions, ignorance and weaken your resolve. Even if for no evil, what do you think people who see you would imagine if you are always in a room or in darkness with your courting partner? "And if another believer is distressed by what you eat, you are not acting in love if you eat it. Don't let your eating ruin someone for whom Christ died." (Rom.14:15 NLT)

THE "TEST RIDE" NONSENSE

You don't get involved before you evaluate.—Dr. Voddie Baucham

For so many years, people with promiscuous tendencies have argued the "test ride" case to justify their fornication. Men especially are guilty of this. They ask, "If you do not test ride a car, how do you know the smoothness of its ride?" This is absolute baloney. The premise of this question is false from its very foundation. Your potential partner is not a car. In fact, none of her features is in any way comparable to a car. She was not manufactured from an automotive factory with a warranty on her, so you cannot just ride her on trial basis. The person you are looking to have as a future spouse is a child of God, not a property.

Many a marriage or relationship fails because one or both partners see the other as a property to own, not a fellow human being to cherish and respect. Some people even treat their cars more respectfully than their partners. That is a shame. Cars have no emotions, no feelings, no blood, soul, or spirit. Cars were not made in the image of God. Stop comparing your partner or would-be partner to a car. You are going to share your life with your partner, not to use her like your car. Do not look for smoothness because she is not a ride. If in the future your partner loses her smoothness, as many cars do over time, are you going to trade her in? Which family would take her back and give you a new one? Do you see the nonsense of the test ride argument as a basis for selecting your future spouse? Your partner is a human being like you with thinking faculties. If you fail to grasp this, you will always have problem keeping a relationship.

Please, my lady readers, know that you were born (not manufactured) with thinking faculties (not software programs). You are dignified, do not allow yourself to be tested like a device. Do not reduce yourself to the level of a simple machine. Since you are a child of God, do not let any man (or woman) deceive you with the test ride nonsense. God made you to standard. He has no question about your body. In fact, the Bible says you were fearfully and wonderfully made. "I praise you because I am fearfully and wonderfully made; your works are wonderful, I know that full well. (Ps. 139:14 NIV). You can say that with David. Everything in you, therefore, should function to God's standards, not to the whims of any selfish person. The test ride argument is the devil's device to encourage fornication in order that the children of God would inaugurate their relationships with an abomination that will haunt them for life. As a child of God, if anyone brings the test ride argument to you, he is literally saying, *Let us sin with our relationship before we submit it to God or even enter into His presence.*" How does that sound to you? Going to God with a gift of sin? Yet, that is really what the person is saying, and you are giving it a thought.

It should sound that wrong in the first place. You should not need even think about an answer. It should be a straight rejection.

Let me draw a parallel between this false argument with what happened in the Garden of Eden just before man's disobedience and subsequent fall. The devil's major weapon against the truth is to sow seeds of doubt in our minds, even of something as clear as a sure statement. In Genesis, God commanded Adam, "but from the tree of the knowledge of good and evil you shall not eat, for in the day that you eat from it you will surely die" (Gen. 2:17 NAS). Eve's preliminary response in Genesis 3:2 shows that she knew this too well. God left no doubt as to the consequences of eating of the tree of the knowledge of good and evil. God was emphatic when He said, "You will *surely* die" (emphasis mine). This is a complete, solid, and unequivocal statement.

Nevertheless, Satan was able to bring about the downfall of our first parents when he enticed them into questioning the truth of God's Word, "Did God *really* say you must not eat the fruit from any of the trees in the garden?" (Gen. 3:1 NLT, emphasis added). In other words, the devil was telling Eve that you cannot trust God entirely for His Word. Note the word *really*. That word is an instrument of doubt. If any man or woman walks up to you and says, "I want you to show me that you are a *real* woman (or man)," quickly cast your mind back to the old serpent. He or she is no different and you know the consequence will not be good if you heed the challenge. If you are a lady, and a man approaches you with this question, tell him to look at your hair, your bust, your curvature, and listen to your voice. If these are not enough to prove to him you are real, not even your nakedness will be sufficient for him. He will jump to another lady as soon as he sees one. It is a certainty, if you fall for a test ride you will become a test bride. You can test your dream car but there is no such thing as test marriage or marriage in experiment. Marriage is a commitment. You are either ready to commit or you are not. On the other hand, if you are a man faced with a similar question from a lady, show her your muscles, your relatively flat chest and body, and ask her to listen to your voice. If the lady is still not convinced of your manhood, she wouldn't be convinced by your nakedness either. She is up to something sinister.

In Genesis, we read, "Then God blessed them and said, "Be fruitful and multiply" (Gen. 1:28 NLT). This makes it clear among other implications that whenever a man and a woman come together, reproduction is a must. If anybody claims not to know this and wants you to prove it before marriage, he or she is up to a ruse. Do not fall for the test ride nonsense. What do you think is the biological significance of men and women in sexual union? By the way, if fertility is your only reason for marriage, you are wrong. There are some people who God intended to be naturally barren or sterile for His purpose. He locked the womb of Sarah and Hannah until further notice for His own purpose. He did the same to Rachel for His own purpose. However, none of these women died a barren. What is important here is to know God's will for you and His timing.

Dr. Myles Munroe made a meaningful comment on Genesis 3:4 in his teaching. The Serpent told Eve that if she ate of the forbidden fruit, she would not die as God had said. But she would rather become like God when in reality they were created in the image of God. They were already like God and needed no one to tell them. In the same way the devil continues to make us doubt what we already are (or have) in order to sell us a counterfeit. The "Test Ride Nonsense" is no different. Dear Ladies, you are already smooth in every part of your body. You do not need to prove it to anybody. Your worth is not in people's opinion. Your worth is in the Creator. What He says about you is what you really are. "But you are a chosen people, a royal priesthood, a holy nation, God's special possession, that you may declare the praises of him who called you out of darkness into his wonderful light."(1 Pet. 2:9 NIV). This is who you are and your purpose.

Before I thought of marriage, I had psyched myself for it. I took inspiration from Shadrach, Meshach and Abednego (Dan. 3:16-18). I sat down and weighed the consequences of the choice I would be making. I trusted God to lead me. Even if He would not, I was ready to live with the consequence of my mistake unto death just like Shadrach, Meshach and Abednego resolved for the sake of their God. I would have no option but to accept the 'mistake' as part of me and learn how to accommodate it. Tinkering with it or running away from it would be the easy but irresponsible way to deal with it. I, therefore, had to confront the issue with boldness, not the indecisive manner of the test ride argument. What you need is principle not a test ride. If you cannot trust God enough to be able to lead you into your future, you are just like the Israelite forefathers who could not trust God to lead them to the promised land in the face of a little adversity (Numbers 21:5). You will pay a price for that. It is simply not worth it.

In his book, "The Fatherhood Principle," Dr. Myles Munroe admonishes men:

"If you are a young man who is dating a young woman, you are to treat her with respect as you would want someone to treat your own daughter. You are not to pressure her into sexual intercourse before marriage. When a woman goes out with a man, she's supposed to feel protected physically, emotionally and spiritually." (The Fatherhood Principle, 2000 p. 38)

"In fact, if a man abuses a woman, he does not know his purpose", he asserts.

DECEPTION AT THE ALTAR

"Be not deceived; God is not mocked: for what-soever a man soweth, that shall he also reap." — Galatians 6:7 (KJV)

Love is patient, and true love truly waits. Unfortunately, many so-called Christian would-be couples do, in fact, know themselves before going to the altar. They fall for the test ride proposition and conclude they like the adventure, so they initiate actions to possess the ride. In effect, God is saying, "Don't do it." You respond, "That does not make sense. I'll do it anyway." So, who is in control here: you or God? Obviously, you have taken the reins in your own hands as a would-be couple. God is no longer in charge. However, after many have test ridden themselves, they then decide to bring their 'ride' before God for consecration. Worse is the fact that the words *Holy Matrimony* appear on their wedding cards. If you have taken God's hand off your partner why tease Him this way? What is so holy about a marriage based on fornication?

Fornication is a serious abomination that requires repentance and confession for subsequent forgiveness. If you are a culprit, welcome to my audience. Who is being deceived here? Clearly, you cannot deceive God, because He saw you even before you came into existence. The only ones you deceived are yourselves, the congregation, and the officiant. If you do not respect God's part in your marriage at all, do not flaunt it in the house of the Holy God. Such false piety does not only constitute a demonstration of lies in the highest form, but it is also an active participation in one of Satan's principal maneuvers—deception. If you are a victim, you need to admit it and ask God for forgiveness. Remember, sin has consequences. "The soul that sinneth, it shall die..." (Ezek. 18:20 KJV)

During a wedding ceremony, the lifting of the veil is symbolic. You are telling the world that this is the first time you are "uncovering" your wife-to-be. The uncovering here is not the literal removing of the veil as we know it—of course, before she was veiled, you saw her physically—but it is symbolic of the fact that you are going to uncover her nakedness for the first time in your life. But if you have already seen everything there is to see about yourselves, what else is there to unveil? What you have to do is to admit your sin before God through confession and ask Him for forgiveness. Then, you can tell your pastor and ask him to marry you in private for that reason. By so doing you are being truthful to God and to yourselves. Your conscience will not judge you. As long as you perpetuate deception at the altar, your sin is ever before you, and the God who sees all things beyond human eyes will one day call you to account. Do not compound your weakness by staging a blatant lie to deceive yourselves and other people. If you cherish marriage or have hopes for a wonderful church wedding, then wait until you go to the altar.

The interesting thing about weddings is that those who fall into temptation do not believe others are genuine. Like themselves, they assume that all other couples are also putting up the same false scheme. In fact, many of the audience at wedding ceremonies are of the view that both the bride and the groom are not as sexually innocent as they portray on stage. If you have already known yourselves, you prove them right and shamefully bring the name of the holy matrimony into disrepute. If you know you cannot be proud of your wedding, do not fake it in the first place. That is why it is important to do whatever it takes to prove those people wrong by being truthful to God and to ourselves before marriage. As believers, let us try not to deceive anybody. Satan is the father of lies and if we join him in that effort, we become like the Pharisees who displayed outward piety but inward rottenness. If Jesus saw through their schemes, He definitely sees through yours as well.

THE MYTH OF SECONDARY VIRGINITY

> *"For if a man think himself to be something, when he is nothing, he deceiveth himself."* — Galatians 6:3 (KJV)

When we talk about virginity, the majority of us focus on ladies. Let me posit that virginity is not limited to women. It extends to gentlemen as well. Men hardly ever think of virginity as a virtue, but it is even more essential to men than it is to women. I am, therefore, not addressing only women in this issue but men as well. As a matter of fact, my focus is even more on men than women. "These are they which were not defiled with *women*; for they are virgins" (Rev. 14:4 KJV, emphasis added). Virginity in the godly sense starts with men. But for the sweet mouths of some men, many women would otherwise be virgins. If we had more virgin men, we would equally have more virgin women.

It is unfortunate that talking about virginity in our present time is rather odd. It used to be the norm in the not-so-distant past. Society has become so permissive and tolerant of sexual immorality that we no longer see anything wrong with it. For those of you who are still bent on keeping your sexual purity, I say, congratulations! Keep the fires burning. You will reap what you sow. I sowed the seed of virginity in myself, and I reaped the rich harvest of love from a virgin woman. That is how it works. "...for whatsoever a man soweth, that shall he also reap." (Gal. 6:7 KJV)

That being said, there is a subtle deception that has gradually made inroads into modern society, even in Christian circles about what is termed secondary virginity. That is the notion that when one breaks his or her virginity at a point in time but abstains from sex for a considerable period of time afterward, he or she somewhat recoups his or her virgin status. This is untrue. You cannot eat your cake and still have it. If we have secondary virginity, then we should have a tertiary one, a fourth, fifth, sixth and virginity becomes valueless, meaningless, and useless. Nobody could be proud of it.

There is no such thing as primary virginity; logically we should not have a secondary one. Virginity is what it is, there is no secondary status to it. The Bible makes mention of virgins but never makes mention of secondary virgins. You are a virgin only once. Virginity is the state of never having had sexual intercourse. Dictionaries are unanimous in their definitions of a virgin: someone who has *never* had sex (emphasis mine). Did you catch the word *never*? It means not ever, not at all, at no time, or on no occasion. So, as soon as you engage in sexual intercourse, you are effectively out of this picture for good. You can abstain for a thousand years afterwards, once you have had sex, you are a veteran. If you are proud of virginity, protect the object of your pride. Do not surrender it needlessly, because once gone, you can never retrieve it. It is like a spoken word. Once it pops off your tongue, you can never retrieve it from the ears that heard it.

What we term secondary virginity is not virginity. I call it being sexually fallow. In farming communities, a virgin forest, one that has never been cultivated or farmed before, loses its fertility over time once cultivated. In order to allow the land to recover some of its fertility and regenerate some of its vegetation, the farmers stop farming it and leave for other lands. Over time, they will return to re-cultivate the same land by which time it would have regrown its vegetation and regained fertility. This process is known as leaving the field fallow in Agricultural Science. However, no matter how many years they allow the land to fallow, it will never recover absolutely as it was untouched. The land will regrow most of its vegetation and recover its fertility to a large extent, but some plant species once noticeable in its pristine days will never be found again. Some animal species that used to live in that forest when it was virgin will never return either. In a fallow forest, you will have a semblance of the original but not the original. If you break your virginity once, you can only console yourself with a fallow not the original.

Am I saying that remaining sexually fallow is bad? Absolutely not! It is next to virginity. If you have surrendered your virginity outside marriage, there is hope for you. Like a fallow land, you will certainly regain some virgin characteristics and that is better than wasting yourself all through prior to marriage. Let me explain this with the parable of the prodigal son. After the younger son had demanded and collected his share of the inheritance, he wasted it and lost everything. That's how one loses his or her virginity. We tell God we want to control our bodies although He created and put us in them. But, when the younger son realized his mistake, what did he do? He thought of going back home (to the original) but he knew within himself that once he had wasted the portion of wealth due him, he could never have it back. Even if his father would accept him back home, his status as an heir may not be the same. He, therefore, contemplated going home to his father not in his capacity as a son but as a hired servant. He said, "I am no longer worthy to be called your son; make me like one of your hired servants.'(Luke 15:19 NIV). The prodigal son really understood what it meant to lose a status. Pride is preventing most of us from accepting our fallen state thus denying us the ability to obtain forgiveness and gain the opportunity for a fresh start.

This notwithstanding, the father was happy to receive him back as a son. Although he clothed him in the best robe, gave him new shoes, put a ring on his finger, and even killed the fattest cow to celebrate his return, one thing remained unchanged. The original portion of the wealth the son took was gone forever. In other words, his virginity was lost forever. Nevertheless, you can be proud in being sexually fallow because when we are counting people who are at present observing abstinence or chastity, you are among them; you are just not a virgin. Like the prodigal son, you can say to your future spouse, "I lost my virginity long ago but after I realized my mistake, I observed chastity for such and such years, all in preparation for you." I assure you, like the father, your spouse would clothe you in the best robes, give you new shoes for your feet, put a ring on your finger, and kill the fattest bull to celebrate your marriage for being truthful and abstaining after losing your virginity. It is not too late. Being sexually fallow is very good, but I would rather be a virgin.

HYMENOPLASTY

Once again, we have heard and perhaps even witnessed or undergone hymenoplasty surgery or hymen repair. Due to technological advancements in medicine, plastic surgeons are able to recreate a woman's hymen using pieces of her body tissues, and it is claimed that the woman regains her virginity. For this reason, this type of surgery is popularly called virginity surgery. This is even more dishonest than the so-called secondary virginity. I will liken it to reforestation. In some places, efforts are made to replant trees on land that used to be a forest. Agricultural scientists call this a reforestation not virgin forest. This means that no matter what you do to recreate nature after destroying it, you can never bring it back to the original. It is so with virginity, and we must accept this as factual. Trying to describe virginity or recreate it in any other way to boost your shattered pride is self-deception.

The hymen is a naturally occurring tissue put in place by the Creator. If you have undergone a hymenoplasty procedure, ask yourself, "who placed your hymen in your vaginal passage?" If it is a physician who sowed an artificial hymen made of your skin tissue to your vaginal passage, then you are not a virgin. Virgin women have no idea how their hymen was placed. If you do know, you are not a virgin. For those who believe in such deceit, I have only one question for you: **If it is not broken, why repair it?**

LOVE DOES NOT MAKE MARRIAGE WORK

> *"The heart is deceitful above all things, and desperately sick; who can understand it?"* — Jeremiah 17:9 (ESV)

When I first heard the above statement from Dr. Myles Munroe, my immediate response was, "How?" I completely disagreed. How can a man of God make such a seemingly contradictory statement? But when I considered his message further, I could not agree with him more. Love as we know it can sometimes be described as a myth. I know many readers will disagree, but before you argue this out as Dr Munroe said, please, find a divorcee and seek his or her impressions about love. Nobody marries a person he or she hates. Divorcees were once head over heels for each other. So, what happened to all that love? Where did it go? The answer to that question explains the mythical nature of what we (humanly) call love.

When love is shattered, its principles shall stand. Let me explain this further. Love toward a spouse has two main components— these are commitment and fascination. Commitment is the core, unconditional principle that underlies love, while fascination is the illusion that clouds it. The illusion is cloudlike, because it has the propensity to dissipate or reform. Unfortunately, many of us see love only in its fascinating form. Is it any wonder, therefore, that we see many marriages go bust?

When the fundamental principle of commitment is missing in a relationship, whatever else remains is an illusion. On the other hand, if the commitment principle is present in a relationship, the fascination may evaporate but the foundation will still be well grounded, always moving the relationship forward until the fascination returns, bringing back the magic. My advice, therefore, is that before your encounters take you down the stairs of love, check to make sure that the fundamental principle of commitment is present and unconditional. If not, the slightest challenge will blow all the cloud away and you will have nothing to hold on to.

Practically, everything in and around you can change except principles. They are constants of life. You may love another person to the core and virtually be willing to die for the fellow. However, certain perturbations arrive and suck out all the affection you have for the person. You could even be married for years, but your partner could look no less an enemy than the devil himself. When that happens, only your principles would keep you going. Therefore, you must not just fall in love, you must embrace a principled love, one founded on commitment.

Many people have ruined their hearts and their relationships because they fell in love. Falling in love suggests an accidental phenomenon, and if you just love by accident, it flies away just as accidentally. It is that simple. If, on the other hand, you love by divine inspiration, that love will be rooted in divine principles of commitment. When the fascination evaporates, the unconditional commitment underlying that love will still remain, and you will find a reason to cling to your partner until the affection returns and it always does. You could be upset or woefully wronged, and your partner may look like the devil. Under such circumstances only your unconditional commitment (principle) will keep you in the relationship. If your marriage or love is accidental, it will not survive the storms of life, because it lacks the fundamental, relevant principle of commitment.

I had the test of my life when Sylvia was denied permission to come with me on a visit. I lost a big chunk of steam in the relationship. I feared Sylvia may not be her own woman in the future. I was worried her father would dictate the pace of our marriage. The last thing I would do is to enter into a marriage covenant only to be micromanaged by a third person. I found no reason to remain in the game. But there was one thing that kept me still going—commitment. It was not for any favor she had done me or favor I sought from her. I had given Sylvia my word, and I was simply committed to it. It was a commitment I made, and I was obliged to keep it or else I would fall into the category of liars. That principle kept us going in the face of disappointment. I have also realized that the commitment principle in love always has an inexplicable element in the twist. To be frank, if you know exactly why you love your partner, and can explain it one hundred percent, you are not quite there yet. On top of the physical attraction, there has to be a non-definable or an inarticulate reason why you want to share your life with that special somebody.

I experienced this during a counseling session with Sylvia's pastor prior to our marriage. I was asked to give my reason(s) why I loved her. To my own shock, I could not give any tangible reason or explain why I loved her. All I felt was that I owed her some unconditional obligation that could not be explained or traced to a physical source. I believe this is the divine (agape) form of love; the element that keeps couples intact in spite of severe challenges. If it is missing in your love relationship, watch your steps for the ground is rough. If you have a reason or an expectation for loving your partner, that reason or expectation becomes a condition, and if your love is based on a condition, guess what happens when that condition is no more? And no condition is guaranteed to be permanent. Wait, therefore, until you can establish an unconditional, divine commitment toward the other person before taking him or her in your love boat for the marriage cruise. Otherwise, when your love boat hits rough seas, you will jettison your partner and be back ashore, at square one. If you just love for loving sake, you will not survive even the slightest storm.

FRIENDSHIP BEFORE RELATIONSHIP

Love is patient and kind . . . It does not demand its own way. — 1 Corinthians 13:4-5 (ESV)

There is a vital ingredient for building a successful marriage relationship that came to us naturally and unconsciously. However, looking back in time, Sylvia and I came to realize that it was always a major contributor to our very decent relationship and successful marriage. This ingredient is friendship. Until I found out that Sylvia would be my future wife, no relationship was intended. Knowing that it would be nearly impossible for us to marry, given our highly contrasting cultural and geographical backgrounds, both of us focused our minds and energies on our partnership specifically the objectives of the partnership. Thus, we began our relationship with shared purpose, motivation, interests, dreams, and personal expectations. Dr Munroe admonishes in his book, *Waiting and Dating* that, "Healthy relationship should always begin at the spiritual and intellectual levels–the levels of purpose, motivation, interests, dreams and personality. (Myles Munroe, 2004 p.13). This made our friendship very strong and healthy. We did not allow physical attraction to feature in the equation. Our emotional involvement didn't appear until quite late, when we knew we were almost a couple. As we kept each other's company and worked together as a team for a common goal, we developed a harmonious telepathy, understanding, respect, and empathy for each other. We came to know each other's weaknesses and strengths. Instead of taking advantage of the other person's weakness, each of us tried to make up for the other's shortcomings as much as possible.

At the same time, we shared a sense of godliness and a penchant for righteousness. Therefore, when we transitioned our study partnership into a personal relationship, it was seamless; there was no friction at all. There is a traditional African adage that goes like this: "Sleep is the simulation of death." Godly friendship is the foundation for a smooth and lasting relationship. If you are not friends before you are a couple, your relationship is bound to suffer stress. To date, the only thing that makes Sylvia and I realize we are a couple is the children we have. Other than that, almost everything else in our lives together is seen through the lens of the friendship we've had. We still partner to work toward our common goals with mutual respect. We observe the same godly principles that defined the foundation of our friendship when we first met. We try to cover up for each other like we did in school. For many occasions, we have had to shake ourselves up to realize we were not just friends but a couple as well. If you take time to build a godly friendship with your partner, it reflects very positively in your relationship. To the glory of God, we have chalked our fourteenth milestone, and there has not been a single brawl in our marriage. Tensions do arise from time to time, but just as we learned to deal swiftly and decisively with them in our friendship, we employ the same arsenal in our marriage. By immersing ourselves in each other's point of view, no matter how silly is seems, we are able to look out for each other with empathy. Sylvia is still my closest and best friend, and that is very reassuring. When you realize that no one else has your best interest more at heart than your closest and best friend who is also your spouse, there will be nothing left in you to hold against him or her. Your anger is quenched and your resentment diminished. Whatever remains will be positive and pure love.

Again, the transparency that existed in our friendship has permeated into our marriage to date. Nothing is hidden between us. If I have to make any request to Sylvia, I do not have to worry about whether she would do it or not. It is a given that so far as it is within her power, it will be done. Neither does Sylvia have to worry about the demands she makes on me for the same reason. The transparency that exists between us gives us a good measure of each other's ability and potential at any point in time. This, in turn, informs the demands we make on each other. Scarcely do we fall short of each other's demands, and scarcely do we demand beyond each other's ability to give.

REMAIN FAITHFUL AND STEADFAST, NO MATTER WHAT

> *If you do not stand firm in your faith, you will not stand at all.* —Isaiah 7:9 (NIV)

We, as mankind, have difficulty with consistency, but to God, consistency is the norm. That is why His love endures forever. However, if we are able to stay faithful to Him even for the slightest period of time, He rewards us greatly. The element of consistency in faithfulness allows God to smoothly roll out His plans for us without having to reschedule or delay them. I have analyzed and come to the conclusion that God planned our union in advance and set it in time. As we stayed faithful to Him, no amount of opposition or impediment could prevent us from ultimately arriving as husband and wife in accordance with His will. I know of at least two officials who fiercely antagonized me because of the way I related to Sylvia. Regardless of their unfounded disapproval, they could not disrupt the cordiality of our friendship. God in His wisdom directed the random paring of students for the internship program to result in the two of us as partners. That, in and of itself, was a divine push. Hardly was it an accident or a coincident.

However, the adverse report sent to the Director of Education about a possible conflict of interest potentially threatened to alter the plan of God for us. Even so, when our pairing was revised, we still ended up in the same school, only we were no longer partners teaching in the same class. Still, man's efforts could never thwart God's plans for us. We were still not very far apart, and we were able to interact at leisure hours. It was in one of these times that Sylvia dropped the Golden Question. God had meant it to be so. He meant to fulfill the conditions spelled out in the covenant through that exercise, and no one could twist His hands. Our faithfulness entrenched God's plan in our lives' events. When He sets the time and season of fulfillment, no one can derail it except yourself. It pays to be faithful no matter what.

THE CHALLENGE OF OTHER WOMEN

*So, if you think you are standing firm, be careful that
you don't fall* — 1 Corinthians 10:12 (NIV)

Right from high school, I had faced and dealt successfully with very challenging issues. After official hours in the boarding house, interactions among cubicle members were often reduced to locker room talks. Most notorious was the period in which we held our Inter-Schools Athletic Competition. That was the only period we were granted blanket exeats to troop to the stadium to cheer our respective athletic teams on to victory. However, that was when students also took advantage to flirt amorously. They would go to clubs, discotheques, and hotels. Whenever they returned in the evening that was the time to recount their sexual and immoral encounters with the opposite sex. They would describe all manner of intimate interactions with their partners among themselves. The best choice I had in such circumstances was to leave the room or struggle to keep my mind from following their conversation. It was always a challenge. Finishing high school was, therefore, a relief for me.

I managed, by the grace of God, to stay away from women for the larger part of my life by consciously pursuing a policy of avoidance. It all went smoothly until the last signal was fulfilled. When I knew who my future wife would be, that was when I started to meet possible alternatives. After 1998, I started making new lady friends in a way I could not understand. Much as I avoided them, I kept bumping into them. Some ladies wrote very challenging letters to me, while others verbally challenged me. The terms of my covenant with God had never been in such danger of violation. The most blatant of these challenges occurred during my mother's funeral in my hometown. The funeral was remarkable as it was very well attended. Auntie Aggie's funeral was likened to a festival due to the unprecedented crowd. Mourners far and near stormed the town on that day due to her popularity.

As they lined up to greet the family members, I was sitting in the midst of my siblings. They started shaking hands with us as custom demanded. The queue elongated from behind. Many people, the majority of whom I did not know, shook our hands. About six ladies in a row greeted us. One of them, in her turn, shook my hands and scratched my palm. I knew exactly what that meant, and it threw me back for a moment. That was a sign of proposal. She had also fulfilled Sign #2. *So, what becomes of Sylvia? How do I know which of them is fake?* This dilemma is what I had always wanted to avoid, hence my resolve to keep my covenant secret. Here I was with these options and with a potential fake from the devil. I needed deep thinking and prayer, and for a moment I lost focus as I thought about what all that meant after all. As I analyzed the situation, I concluded that, this lady was the fake one, not Sylvia. First, this lady fulfilled Sign #2 all right, but in a manner that was inappropriate. She was not looking for life's commitment as Sylvia did. She was seeking to fornicate. This is what believers must know. As much as God has good plans for us, the enemy also has his own counter productive plans for us. By the time the true one from God arrives, you might have already been neck deep in a troubled choice. That is why the spirit of discernment is vital for all believers. We need to be able to sift out the fake from the real. We can only do this if we are in tune with the Holy Spirit. Other than that, I see no other way. I decided not to look at this questionable lady a second time, let alone ascertain specifically who she was. As of now, I still have no idea who she was, neither could I recognize her if I should meet her today. I continued shaking hands with those offering their condolences as if nothing had happened. I also knew it was a danger zone for me, so I did not waste time sneaking out earlier than the usual closing time. I did not want whoever she was to approach me a second time. I needed to do three things urgently.

First of all, to me, that was a spiritual threat, and I had to do whatever it took to stay away as far as possible. Second, I had already given Sylvia my word and abandoning her would have amounted to a grave betrayal and deception. I would have been a first-class liar, and Sylvia would have suffered a broken heart. If I had made a mistake, I was going to stay committed to her as I had already established in my principle beforehand. Third, that lady was looking for instant sensual gratification through sex. She would have seduced me to violate my covenant and guess what the consequences would have been? It was simply not worth it.

WHEN GOD IS SILENT, HE IS STILL WORKING

"Through faith we understand that the worlds were framed by the word of God, so that things which are seen were not made of things which do appear." — Hebrews 11:3 KJV

Have you ever reached a point in your life when you really needed to hear from God, yet there was absolute silence from His end? You are among the many believers who have gone through it. Unfortunately, some could not endure and desperately listened to another voice instead. In his book, *Rules of Engagement,* Derek Prince observes that if God withdraws His presence and does not seem to be active in your life, it can mean that He is testing you to see how you will behave when left to yourself. (Derek Prince, 2006, p. 60). Let me assure you, when God is silent, He is busily working on your behalf. You have to wait for Him even if it feels like you are losing. Do you remember Saul arrogating to himself the duty of a priest in a mounting challenge of the Philistine army? Well, that was the major blunder that cost him the throne in the sight of God. (See 1Sam. 13). God is not obliged to answer every call of ours, but He is bound by every Word of His concerning us.

Joseph had a similar experience in Potiphar's house. (See Genesis 39:7-20 for the full story). He was, in fact, the victim of a rape attempt, but Mrs. Potiphar flipped the story making Joseph the aggressor. This was clearly an unfair situation given the consequence. I have no doubt Joseph expected God to intervene—you and I would think the same. After all, Joseph was preserving himself for God, yet, God looked on while Joseph was sentenced to prison. Where was God? Absolutely silent! Did it mean He had abandoned Joseph? Absolutely not! He was seriously organizing developments to furnish Joseph with management expertise and almost superhuman interpretation skills. God used the prison as the platform for this. God was busily working on his behalf and for his future. Going through hard times is a problem for us but nothing before God. He knows He can remove your difficulty at any moment, but it might just be your training tool. If you need the training therein contained, He will not get you out in a hurry. So, be still and endure for now. You will come out refined, better and singing in the end.

THE VALUE OF SECRECY

"Even a fool who keeps silent is considered wise;
when he closes his lips, he is deemed intelligent."
—Proverbs 17:28 (ESV)

A secret is of much value. Its indispensability cannot be overemphasized. If not, the world's intelligence services would not exist as vital state machinery to their various governments. It is as true with individuals as it is with governments. Do not trash secrets or give them away easily. Secrecy is a powerful tool for controlling your world.

Proverbs says, "Whoever guards his mouth preserves his life; he who opens wide his lips comes to ruin" (Prov. 13:3 ESV). This should tell you how valuable secrecy is to life. It is the kingpin of life. Most wisdom is habored in secrecy. If you will ever be destroyed, it is because you opened your mouth too wide. You gave out the vitality of your life. That is why you were left helpless. Bruce Barton, a famous advertiser once said, "For good or for ill, your conversation is your advertisement. Anytime you open your mouth, you allow the world to look into your mind." This means if you do not keep some things to yourself, but choose to blurt out every issue in your mind and about your life, you allow others to easily predict you. Once people can accurately anticipate your next move, you are doomed. They can control you. You become helpless as every move of yours can be thwarted. If your efforts are thwarted, you become vulnerable and subdued.

Why did God tell Abraham to leave his country, kindred, and family in Genesis 12? Because He wanted to reveal a secret to him. God told Abraham to leave to a land that He would show him. Why did God not give Abraham the message straight away while he was among his family members? Some things are meant just for you alone. No one else needs to hear it, at least for a given time period. It was not until Abraham reached the land of Canaan that God appeared to him again and said, "Yes, this is the land that I was talking about" (Gen. 12:7 author's paraphrase). God would not even describe it to Abraham while he was still in his father's house. He showed him only when he had left and was alone. God also loves secrets.

We keep discovering new galaxies, species of animals, chemical elements, and other matters of nature. Why did God not reveal them from the beginning but hid them for man to discover at later dates? Some things are for a particular season. That is why you must keep some things to yourself until very deep in the future when they are due to be let out in their season. The intelligence community calls this declassification. It did not start with the CIA, the KGB, or the MOSSAD. It originated with the Maker of the Universe Himself, and we must learn from Him.

The latter part of Revelations 13:8 refers to Jesus as the Lamb slain (or slaughtered) from the foundation of the world. This shows that God's plan of salvation was not an afterthought. He did not think it up after the fall of man. He knew what the devil would do, so He had it covered right from the beginning of His creation work—long before Satan nursed the idea of sabotaging God's work in his mind. When did God reveal His salvation plan? It became clear only when He was about to execute it through Jesus Christ. Many of the prophets through whom God announced Christ's coming did not even know exactly how and when. He sneaked into the world in a sheep pen while the world was expecting a political, majestic and flamboyant entry. Apart from Mary and Joseph, all other witnesses of His appearance were animals, sheep to be precise. Imagine if the devil had a hint of this idea. He would never have stirred anybody against Christ, let alone think about killing Him. As a result, God's plan of salvation would have come to naught. This is why the apostles continually referred to Christ as "The Mystery of God" (1 Cor. 2:7-9; Col. 2:2-3; 1:27; Eph. 1:9-10; Titus 1:3, 1 Peter 1:10-12; 20). A mystery is knowledge that exists in secret and is only guaranteed by secrecy. As soon as a mystery is unwrapped from secrecy, it becomes a common knowledge as the mysteriousness of that wisdom evaporates with the revelation. The Creator valued secrecy and employed it in His work. How much more should we, His children, value it in our own lives? I wonder why we are able to keep our sins very secret but cannot shut our mouths on our good deeds and intentions. I think it should be the other way round. We should keep quiet about our good works and intentions but confess our sins and wrongdoings.

From the beginning, the value of secrecy was not lost on me. Introverts are natural custodians of secrets, and I had a natural ability to keep secrets. I was born that way for a reason. Never despise your personality orientation. It may be unpleasant for others but God meant it for good for your sake. I refused to open my mouth in order that I may keep my covenant between me and my God. No amount of pressure would force me to divulge information on that. This is what Samson failed to do, which cost him his strength and eventually his life. He failed to keep his secret to himself. As soon as he revealed it to Delilah, he was doomed. If, from the beginning, I stressed secrecy, it was worth it. As we have already learned from Proverbs 13:3, your secret is your life. When people cannot predict you, they will fear you. They may openly hate you and call you all sorts of names, but in their hearts, they fear your next move. Do not give in to the pressure of name calling. You are in control, and that is what matters. Once you lose momentum, you will be controlled.

THE WILDERNESS

> *"My brethren, count it all joy when ye fall into diverse temptations; knowing this, that the trying of your faith worketh patience."* —James 1:2-3 (KJV)

The wilderness is a good training ground for spiritual maturity. There, one gets furnished with the right tools and experiences required for the battle ahead. I could never suspect or imagine that my ability to pass the A Level exam was, in fact, divinely tied to establishing my acquaintance with Sylvia. My struggle with the "A" Level exam was an act of God to slow me down so that she could catch up with me. My future wife was far behind me academically, but God had intended us to meet at a certain point in time to make His plan come true for us "For I know the plans that I have for you. . . , plans to prosper you and not to harm you, plans to give you hope and a future" (Jer. 29:11). I saw it as distress, struggle, and a hustle. In fact, God meant it for my own good, just as Joseph's imprisonment was for his good. If I had known His intentions for me, I would have faced it with a smile.

One thing we learn from this is that God has a lot of promises for us, but when it comes to their fulfillment, He does not usually give us the exact details about how and when He is going to carry them out. This is where our patience and loyalty are tested and our faith is tried. Our curiosity and impatience hurry us toward needless conclusions and the acceptance of mediocrity. We may know about God's promises for us all right, but the how, the where, and the when are lost on us. There is nothing so intriguing to man than such a situation. We simply have to be patient and wait for God's timing. He who promised knows how, when, and where to fulfil it. Do not insert yourself into it or your impatience will mislead you to short-circuit God's purposes for you and others. While we may put various twists to God's purposes, we usually get it wrong. Let us consider a few instances in the Bible where man's thinking contrasted with God's purpose. Take the story of David for instance. When his father, Jesse, sent him to give food to his soldier brothers, both father and son were thinking solely in terms of an errand, but God had a different agenda for David. He wanted to glorify Himself through David. If you happened to be in Bethlehem and had asked Jesse where David was at that time, he would have responded, "I have sent him to deliver food supplies to his brothers at the war front." If you happened to chase David and caught up with him, he would have told you he was on his way to deliver food and provisions to his three brothers in Saul's Army. Remarkably, if you had approached God and asked of David's whereabouts, you would be surprised at His response. He would have told you, "I have sent him to go and fight." Indeed, no sooner had David arrived at the site of battle than he plunged into the fight with Goliath and surprisingly won. God used the errand as a pretext; the real motive was known only to Him. God is under no obligation to explain Himself to anybody. He does so when and to whom He chooses.

Who can question Him? Again, let us consider Rebecca on the day Abraham's servant arrived at the well. She was taking her father's flock to pasture which was a routine for her. To her, it was business as usual. Hardly did she know that she would return home a wife. If anybody familiar with Rebecca was asked who she was, the answer would be unanimous — a shepherd girl. But if anybody had approached God early that day with the same question, His answer would have been, "She is Isaac's wife". In a similar fashion, God prompted Kish to send his son, Saul, to look for missing asses, yet God had the ultimate mission for Saul. God had already revealed Saul's arrival to Samuel the previous day, leading to his eventual anointing and enthronement. When the divine mission was accomplished, the asses were found.

In the same way, as soon as I had established a relationship with Sylvia, a divine mission, I passed the "A" Level with flying colors. Sylvia and I both graduated from Mount Mary College in 1998 and just the following year in 1999, I passed the "A" Level with distinction. That was not by accident. For the nine years prior that I had struggled, trying to get into the University; nothing worked for me. At this point in time all avenues closed to me except the pathway to the Training College. Work and life's conditions became so unbearable that the only way out was to take that path. How come when I took it and made contact with Sylvia, everything came at my beck and call? Multiple pathways to the university opened for me. I could opt for virtually any course and was sure to be accepted. Divine inspiration cannot be discounted in this matter. God had plans for me and was making sure I did not overshoot or lag behind in His scheme of affairs. If you surrender your will to God, He takes charge of your life, and never will He let you down. Even if you do not know where the ship of your life is drifting as my days in the 'wilderness', you should know who is in charge. That alone should give you enough confidence to stabilize your life until the fulfillment of His plans for you.

Many a time we think we are pursuing our own dream, but God mysteriously lands us on another project we have never even considered. It all happens in the wilderness where no hope is in sight. You may meet your Goliath there or lose all hope of making it. You may not understand why certain things do not bode well for you in a certain arena. It is at these times that you must stay put and endure, for in His time He will make all things beautiful. You will either forget your past suffering or remember it with fondness.

COUNT YOUR BLESSINGS

If it had not been the LORD who was on our side—
let Israel now say. —Psalm 124:1 (NKJV)

If you do not count your blessings, the devil will always give you something else to count, but eventually you will not be happy with it. I failed to understand this for a while. When I finally broke through the "A" Level exam, I was cheered up but only briefly. I mostly kept a quiet demeanor, because in my thoughts it was long overdue. Some of my colleagues had finished their master's and doctoral degree courses by then. I was just going to begin my bachelor's, not my masters so I would not even be close. Looking at things from this perspective made my success look like trash, as if it was nothing to be proud of. I could not count my blessings. Passing the "A" Level was something I'd worked hard for and prayed hard about, and I was happy to have conquered at last. However, it is one thing being successful and another thing being grateful or thankful for it. I was elated for the triumph, but I was looking at it from the wrong perspective, which prevented me from appreciating it and learning that God had dealt well with me. I sat for the exam with hundreds of other students, many of whom did not pass, yet that was the last exam of that kind to be ever taken. What if I had fallen into that category? Furthermore, I came to acknowledge the value of the delay at the "A" Level only after we married. I realized that I had been marking time to meet my future wife without whom life would have been unbearable. Always count your blessings, and you will really come to appreciate the vital provisions of God everybody else takes for granted. You will be thankful.

NO EASY GAME

> *Joyful is the person who finds wisdom, the one who gains understanding.* —Proverbs 3:13 (NLT)

I found that keeping the relationship going while keeping Sylvia unawares of proceedings was one of the most difficult aspects to manage. While I was seeing things by the book, Sylvia had no clue what I was seeing or looking at. While I had hindsight, she knew not the role she was playing in the whole scheme of affairs. While she wanted us to talk more about our possible future union, I was rather non-communicative, calm, comfortable, and mostly just observant as things were rolling out in fulfillment of my covenant terms. The different perspectives from which we operated led to a situation where Sylvia sometimes got confused and frustrated. My calm demeanor and long silences made her wonder if I was genuinely interested in the relationship at all.

Sometimes, I felt pushed to reveal or explain things to her in order to reassure her, but I restrained myself. The covenant was enacted in absolute secrecy. Keeping it secret, therefore, was a major provision to determine the validity of proceedings. I felt that if I did anything to influence Sylvia's behavior, I would invalidate the divine yardstick with which I was measuring every step. I did not want to twist Sylvia's hand in my favor. I had a firm belief that if God had started this, He was going to finish it no matter how or when. He would not need my help in this. What I needed to do was to focus on God and watch my checklist to see if Sylvia's behavior still aligned with the terms of the covenant. If Sylvia was the devil's deception, she would deviate from the terms of the covenant, and it would show. In that case, it would be better for me if she left the relationship. I took a hardline position and was determined to tell her about the three main provisions of the covenant only if and after we succeeded in marrying. Thank God, that in spite of the uncertainties, Sylvia did not feel as comfortable with anybody else as she did with me. So, she was forced to go along with me in whatever it took. I am grateful to God Sylvia listened to His voice and did not give in to all those rich and powerful men who came to ask for her hand in marriage. While they paraded many promises and wealth before her, I had nothing but advice for her. My wish was for her to get her bachelor's to enhance her future prospects and be on the same level with me before marriage. "Even if you choose to marry someone else, finish your bachelor's first," I advised. Wise as she is, Sylvia saw that as very unselfish and well-meaning. She recognized that I was not only interested in her body but in her person and future empowerment as well. "That is the man to go with," she reckoned. Your desire for your partner must go beyond body, wealth, and position. You should not see him or her as another person other than you. You must seek out his or her welfare just like you would want for yourself. The difference here was that, while the other men gave Sylvia a sight to see, I placed before her a vision to perceive. It was a heart versus head matter. Sight is a function of the eyes, but vision is a function of both the mind and the heart. I appealed to Sylvia's mind and heart instead of her eyes and pride, so she had no difficulty in knowing which way to go. As a true believer, Sylvia opted to walk by faith instead of sight.

Please, my sisters in Christ, look for men who will give you a vision not those who parade wealth before your eyes in order to convince you. If money and wealth becomes your attraction for marriage, your marriage will collapse when they are no more.

"For everything in the world—the lust of the flesh, the lust of the eyes, and the pride of life—comes not from the Father but from the world. The world and its desires pass away, but whoever does the will of God lives forever." (1 John 2:16-17 NIV)

MARRIAGE PREPARATION

But he said to me, "My grace is sufficient for you, for my power is made perfect in weakness." —2 Corinthians 12:9 (ESV)

I would also like to share with you my experience in marriage preparations and this goes particularly to the men. I realized in mine that no matter how much I prepared, there was always one thing left that I wanted done before marriage. I never felt adequately prepared. That feeling was always there. Every day, there will be a twist to your plans and you will want to make room for the pleasant new idea. By the time you finish implementing one idea, another five will have run in. If you keep making room for idea after idea, by the time you lift up your eyes, your bride-to-be will be approaching menopausal age. The truth is that one simply can never prepare adequately enough for marriage. You just have to prepare enough and get going. The rest will fall into place afterward. Two heads are better than one. Much as you want to please your future partner in the wedding, do not forget that she (or he) will feel much fulfilled by contributing fully to the overall success of your lives. Make room for your partner's role. She or he will appreciate it.

Lightning Source UK Ltd.
Milton Keynes UK
UKHW020735130220
358658UK00001B/2